JACK, JOSEPH AND MORTON MANDEL
SCHOOL OF APPLIED SOCIAL SCIENCES

Case Western Reserve
UNIVERSITY

Jack, Joseph and Morton Mandel School of Applied Social Sciences

100 YEARS of Inspiring Hope and Shaping the Future

Elise C. Hagesfeld, MNO, PhD
with Elizabeth Salem, PhD

Orange *frazer* Press
Wilmington, Ohio

ISBN 978-1939710-789
Copyright©2018 Jack, Joseph, and Morton Mandel
School of Applied Social Sciences

Published for Jack, Joseph, and Morton Mandel
School of Applied Social Sciences by:
Orange Frazer Press
P.O. Box 214
Wilmington, OH 45177
Telephone: 937.382.3196 for price and shipping information.
Website: www.orangefrazer.com

All photos are from Case Western Reserve University and
Mandel School archives unless otherwise noted.

Book and cover design: Alyson Rua and Orange Frazer Press

Library of Congress Control Number: 2018935381

Printed in China

First Printing

IN GRATITUDE

We are grateful to the Jack, Joseph and Morton Mandel Foundation for making this book possible. For more than 50 years, their unwavering and visionary support has helped our School create thousands of leaders in social change who are transforming countless individuals, communities, and nations.

+ Joseph, Morton and Jack Mandel *(Nannette Bedway)*.

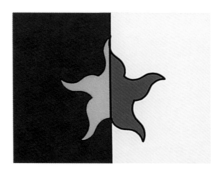

+ Heraldic school banner for official Case
Western Reserve University ceremonies.

OUR MISSION

Advancing leadership in social work and nonprofit education, scholarship, and service to build a more just world.

OUR VISION

Students are central in all that we do, and they actively participate and contribute to a dynamic learning community that develops leaders of social change in direct practice, community practice, and nonprofit management.

The Mandel School was founded by and for the Greater Cleveland community in the belief that a university-based school of social work would transform the work of people and organizations to achieve to their full potential. As the Mandel School celebrates its centennial, we reaffirm our historical commitment to the application of social science for improving social welfare, and seek to continue to broaden the national and international reach of our research, teaching, and service. Our graduates are prepared to be future leaders who turn knowledge into action that furthers health, well being, and social justice.

+ Class of 1952.

CONTENTS

Creating Leaders in Social Change for 100 Years

+ Barbara R. Snyder, JD

In 1915, the United States had not yet entered World War I, and the country was moving from an agrarian to an industrial economy. With more people moving into urban areas, American cities also were struggling to meet the social and cultural needs of their neediest residents. It was no coincidence that 1915 was also the year that Western Reserve University founded the first university-affiliated professional graduate school of social work in the country—the School of Applied Social Sciences.

In 1915, Western Reserve University's president was Charles Thwing[1], and the University was in the midst of expanding its academic offerings. The City of Cleveland's population had increased considerably, and it was grappling with how to provide basic services to its most vulnerable citizens.

This marked the beginning of a strong partnership between the School of Applied Social Sciences and the city as well as solidifying Western Reserve University's role as an urban university committed to serving its local community. President Thwing and James Cutler, sociology department chair and later the school's first dean, were unwavering advocates in establishing a social work school, and in 1916, the school welcomed its first class of 35 students.

Today, the Jack, Joseph and Morton Mandel School boasts over 600 students and its master's degree program is ranked number nine in the U.S. Each year, its students contribute more than 225,000 hours of community service in Northeast Ohio and beyond. Its research grant funding has increased by 270 percent since 2005. It set a school record of winning $9.4 million in research and training grants in 2015 and 2016. Like a century ago, the Mandel School's faculty, staff and students are advancing research on pressing issues facing our society, such as violence prevention and intervention, child maltreatment, alcohol and other drug abuse, community development, and criminal justice—the school responds to these community needs through training, technical assistance, and program evaluation.

The Mandel School has enjoyed a significant relationship with the Jack, Joseph and Morton Mandel Foundation, whose hallmark is "investing in people with the values, ability, and passion to change the world." They have done just that, including through a profound impact on our campus. Gifts from the brothers, their family foundations or their former company, Premier Industrial Cor-poration, have created numerous student scholarships, funded vital research, endowed professorships, and since 1988, they have given their family name to the Mandel School.

Once again, in 2013, the Mandel Foundation provided an extraordinary gift of $9.2 million for the transformative renovation and addition to the Mandel School's main building. Opened during the school's centennial celebration, this renovation reflects and accommodates the innovative ways that Mandel School faculty teach and conduct research and how its students learn. It gives them space to interact, meet the needs of its team-oriented research centers, and encourage increased collaboration in teaching and learning.

In its first one hundred years, the Mandel School defined and advanced the field of social work. I am confident the school will continue its excellent research, teaching and innovation to meet the challenges of the next century and will remain a treasured gem within Case Western Reserve University.

BARBARA R. SNYDER, JD
President
Case Western Reserve University

1 Case Western Reserve President Charles Thwing was among the 60 leaders who signed the founding document establishing the National Association for the Advancement of Colored People (NAACP).

+ Dean Grover C. Gilmore, PhD

Inspiring Hope. Shaping the Future.

When I became Dean of the Jack, Joseph and Morton Mandel School of Applied Social Sciences in 2002, I immediately appreciated the long history of innovation in education that had characterized the Mandel School to that point and how that legacy would demand a lot from me and the faculty in the years ahead.

In those early days, I would attend national meetings of major leadership organizations, like the Council on Social Work Education or the Association for Research on Nonprofit Organizations and Voluntary Action, and would hear of our reputation as a school involved at all levels—from the dean to faculty members and professional staff—in shaping dialogs and making an impact on education and the fields of social work and nonprofit management.

We've been making an impact since December 4, 1915. That's when the School of Applied Social Sciences, as it was known then, was started at the request of community leaders representing 18 social and civic organizations who recognized the benefits of investing in services for all people in order to build a strong community. By this action more than 100 years ago, the first university-affiliated professional graduate school of social work in the United States was established at what was then Western Reserve University.

That was the first of very many highlights that mark more than a century of being a pioneering School in a pioneering field, with innovations that put the school at the forefront of education and in the fields of social work and nonprofit management.

The School created the first group work curriculum in 1923, and group work innovator and social work icon Grace Longwell Coyle joined the faculty in 1934, further bolstering the school's commitment to innovation in group work. In the 1950s, the Mandel School created the first social-science based curriculum that became the model for all social work education while also being one of the first schools in the country to establish a doctoral program in social welfare.

When few schools of any kind were interested in teaching about substance abuse, the Mandel School stepped up and established a highly regarded curriculum specialization in alcohol and other drugs (AODA) in 1976, receiving more than $16 million in grants since to train thousands of social work students, licensed professionals and faculty members.

And when accessibility to a master's degree in social work for older, employed social workers was basically nonexistent, the school responded by developing the first intensive weekend master's program for employed social workers in 1985, basing it on an adult-learning model.

The innovations didn't stop there. Case Western Reserve founded one of the first nonprofit management graduate programs in America in 1989. The Mandel School created the first competency-based social work education model in 2002, known as Ability-Based Learning Environment (ABLE), based on eight core learning outcomes or abilities. ABLE set new standards for professional social work education. The Council on Social Work Education (CSWE) established standards for outcome-based education for all accredited social work programs in 2008, with its 10 competencies having direct linkages to ABLE's eight abilities.

The school has also embraced technology to improve learning, including using web-based technology for the teaching of social work practice in 2011 and launching an 100% online format of the Master of Science in Social Administration (MSSA) degree in 2013.

In celebrating the Mandel School's Centennial in 2015 and 2016, we had many opportunities to reflect on the storied history of the school and its impact, its present place and our vision for the future. One constant remains: A commitment to creating leaders in social change who will make the world a more just place.

What will the next 100 years of innovation and accomplishments look like? As a behavioral scientist, I know the best way to predict the future is to look to the past. And that past has a stellar trajectory. And I also know that whatever the future holds, the Mandel School is going to be there—challenging others and producing new knowledge that will impact policies and practices.

So, it's easy to predict that future, because I know the past. Our Centennial celebration message is what the Mandel School will carry forward for the next century as we continue transforming communities and people's lives: Inspiring hope. Shaping the future.

GROVER C. GILMORE, PhD
Jack, Joseph and Morton Mandel Dean
in Applied Social Sciences
Professor of Psychology and Social Work

The Connection to History and Community

The establishment of the Jack, Joseph and Morton Mandel School of Applied Social Sciences occurred during one of the most significant decades in Cleveland's history. It was a period in which the city's population rose to the fifth-highest in the nation and Cleveland became solidly positioned as a major center of industry and commerce. More importantly, the 1910s marked the high point of the Progressive Era in Cleveland. Because of the mayoralty (1901–1909) of Tom L. Johnson, Cleveland had a tradition of forward-looking good government which was continued by his acolyte, Newton D. Baker, mayor from 1912 to 1916. Progressive urban maturity brought about the creation of a number of organizations that endure today, among them the City Club, the Cleveland Museum of Art, the Cleveland Founda-

tion, the Metroparks system, Karamu House, and the Cleveland Play House. All, including the School of Applied Social Sciences (or SASS, as the Mandel School was called then), were, in one way or another, dedicated to improving the lives of those who lived in the city.

It is tempting to see this period as a golden era, but that is not fully the case. There were numerous problems inherent in Cleveland's rise to what might be considered urban adulthood. By 1920, Cleveland was overcrowded, its air polluted, and its schools unable to properly meet the needs of an industrial metropolis. More than anything else, the issues that faced the community centered on people—the vast growing population that provided labor for the industries. Two-thirds of its population was of foreign birth or foreign parent-

+ John J. Grabowski, PhD

age and another 35,000 were African American, most of whom had recently arrived as part of the first "Great Migration." The world they lived in was absent job security and safety, often absent adequate housing, and in many ways alien.

The creation of SASS thus did not occur in a vacuum. It also followed on national efforts to transform what was once simply known as "charity" into an organized, rational method of dealing with the nation's social needs. The School's task was to educate social workers so they could understand the roots of the problems that occurred in families, neighborhoods, and communities and determine how best to ameliorate them. The process was not then, nor is it now, confined to the classroom and research library. It involved one-to-one connections by faculty and students with the community and the social agencies that served it. While one might conclude that the community simply served as the laboratory for the School, the records that trace its evolution argue for a closer, more personal bond, one implicit in the humanistic motivation that has attracted students and faculty to the School since the day it opened. This combination of the personal and professional allowed the School to innovate in areas such as group work and to sense new issues challenging the fabric of the community. By doing so, it set standards recognized throughout the field of social work.

Today, this sense of mission and focus on innovation remain the core of the Mandel School. Its faculty and students have investigated, worked within, and advocated for the city and region's population through wars, the Great Depression, urban crises, a changing demography, and economic shifts, including those attendant on the current "deindustrialization" and "reinvention" of Cleveland. That story of individual and professional commitment is central to this anniversary history of the Jack, Joseph and Morton Mandel School of Applied Social Sciences which, for a century, has served as Case Western Reserve's most visible connection to the wider community that is its home.

JOHN J. GRABOWSKI, PhD
*Krieger-Mueller Associate Professor of
    Applied History*
Case Western Reserve University

*Historian and Senior Vice President for
    Research and Publications*
Western Reserve Historical Society

Editor
Encyclopedia of Cleveland History

Jack, Joseph and Morton Mandel School of Applied Social Sciences

100 YEARS of Inspiring Hope and Shaping the Future

1914

World War I begins

1916

President Woodrow Wilson is reelected

1918

Worldwide influenza epidemic

1922

Cleveland's first radio station, WHK, begins broadcasting

1929

Stock market crashes, beginning the Great Depression

Germans sink *Lusitania*, killing 128 Americans

1915

Mary Richmond publishes her seminal book on social case work, *Social Diagnosis*

1917

Ratification of the 19th Amendment, granting women the right to vote

1920

Charles Lindbergh flies solo across the Atlantic Ocean

1927

CHRONOLOGY 1910–1929

CHAPTER 1

Answering the Cry of the Community

The history of the founding of the Jack, Joseph, and Morton Mandel School of Applied Social Sciences is linked directly to the history of the city of Cleveland, Ohio. Born of the interplay between community needs, university engagement, and a passion for social justice, the School—like its hometown—was one of the great innovators in the field of philanthropy and social service, at the nexus of national and international conversations about how to best address the most pressing problems of a modern, industrialized America.

Rapid Growth and Growing Needs

In the early 20th century, Cleveland was on the rise. The city drew immigrants from across the country and the world to work in its factories. Standard Oil, Sherwin Williams, U.S. Steel, and other industrial giants were at the cutting edge of manufacturing technology. Between 1900 and 1930, the city's population more than doubled, from about 382,000 to 900,000 people. It was home to two prestigious universities, Western Reserve University and Case School of Applied Science—both conduits for ideas, innovation, and experimentation.

As the city grew, it became more ethnically, racially, and religiously diverse. The first settlers of Cleveland were New Englanders, the British, and German Jews. In the mid-nineteenth century, the Irish came. In the great wave of immigration to the United States between 1879 and 1925, Cleveland also became home to significant populations of Italians, Czechs, Slovaks, Slovenes, Austro-Hungarians, Russians, and Jewish immigrants from across Eastern Europe. The city became a haven for African Americans leaving the Jim Crow South and seeking economic and social opportunities in northern cities.

Cleveland's rapid development was not entirely positive. The influx of people overwhelmed the existing infrastructure, creating housing shortages and overcrowded, unsanitary living conditions. Tuberculosis and pneumonia were endemic. Unskilled laborers and their families struggled to get out of poverty, hampered by boom and bust economic cycles which left people out of work for extended periods. The families of immigrant laborers clustered in ethnic neighborhoods, and African-American families were limited to housing in the few neighborhoods that would rent to blacks. The result was a city divided by a river, ethnicity, race, and opportunity—where children were just

+ Cleveland Public Square, the bustling heart of a progressive metropolis, in 1916 *(Cleveland Picture Collection, Cleveland Public Library).*

+ James F. Jackson, 1926 *(Western Reserve Historical Society).*

as likely to be in the labor force as in school, and where public, religious, social, and charitable institutions struggled to create a cohesive sense of community. The leaders of the city began to fear that, in the midst of growing prosperity, a permanent underclass was being created.

A Charitable Driving Force

With a drive toward creating efficiencies in charitable giving through "scientific philanthropy," Cleveland's business leadership founded Associated Charities in 1904. Its first General Secretary, James F. Jackson, would lead the organization until 1927 and play a pivotal role in the foundation of a school of social work that used the city as its teacher and its laboratory.

Jackson was a graduate of the New York School of Philanthropy. He arrived in Cleveland from Minnesota, where he had worked for similar agencies and had been Secretary of the State Board of Charities and Corrections. Jackson initiated training courses for Associated Charities staff in social work methods, and they provided direct services, including food relief, shelter for the homeless, job training, and support for single mothers. They also coordinated a central registry and employed "friendly visitors" to assess the needs of those applying for relief.

In 1913, perceiving the need for further organization, Associated Charities collaborated with the Jewish Community Federation and leaders from the Chamber of Commerce to create the Cleveland Federation for Charity and Philanthropy, which coordinated fundraising activities across multiple social service agencies, as well as holding those agencies to rigorous standards in explaining their work, their budgets, and their outcomes. Informally, it came to be called the Community Chest—the predecessor of the United Way.

So deeply did Cleveland's leadership invest in this model that an observer writing for *The New Republic* in the 1920s noted: "To flout the Community Chest in Cleveland would be like refusing to stand at attention at West Point while the national anthem is being played. It simply isn't done. The result is what might mildly be described as a centralization of charitable and uplifting activities."

Community Petitions for a Social Work School

One of the results of this centralization was that agencies under review by the Cleveland Federation for Charity and Philanthropy began to approach Jackson at Associated Charities for help in training their own workers. Because Western Reserve University faculty were active in the leadership of many community organizations, it seemed only logical to turn to the University itself for help with such an ambitious project.

In December 1913, Jackson—together with Martin Marks, Director of the Cleveland Federation for Charity and Philanthropy, and Dr. A.R. Warner of Lakeside Hospital and Western Reserve Uni-

versity Medical School–drafted a petition to the Western Reserve University Board of Trustees that was signed by eighteen community organizations requesting the formation of a social work school. The petitioners were public and private agencies providing health and human services across the city, and they were pleading for help in training their workers for service in diverse and demanding roles. The petitioners included:

+ Alta House.

- Cleveland settlement houses Alta House, Hiram House, and Goodrich House;
- Healthcare providers such as Cleveland City Hospital (today known as The MetroHealth System), Lakeside Hospital (University Hospitals), Babies' Dispensary and Hospital (Rainbow Babies and Children's Hospital), and the Visiting Nurse Association; and
- Social service providers including Associated Charities (which became the Centers for Families and Children), the Cleveland Federation for Charity and Philanthropy (Center for Community Solutions and United Way), and the YWCA.

The petition asked the trustees to consider that recent demand for social service workers

was exceeding the ability of philanthropic institutions to provide even short-term training, and that Western Reserve University "has the necessary standing and prestige to attract properly prepared students to sociologic courses carrying university credits and leading to degrees. Reserve also has the confidence and friendship of every social institution of Cleveland, so that practical extension courses could be given in cooperation with each and all of such institutions, and opportunity given to prepare for any special field of work."

While the trustees were deliberating, the first of eight community surveys by the newly-founded Cleveland Foundation—America's first community foundation—recommended that one way to increase the efficiency in administration and service delivery of charitable organizations was to recruit more and better trained social workers. James E. Cutler, who was chair of the sociology department at the University, had already begun to provide extension courses for employees of the Visiting Nurse Association. University faculty began to warm to the idea of creating a school of social work.

On October 24, 1914, Western Reserve University trustees established "The School of Social Sciences and Research." That's when the real work began. In late 1914, trustee William H. Baldwin visited New York City and consulted with John M. Glenn and Mary Richmond of the Russell Sage Foundation—both pioneers of the early professionalization of social work—regarding the organization of the new school. During this trip, he and fellow board member J.B. Chamberlain also met with Cutler, who was visiting New York on a research trip. Baldwin was favorably impressed, and he recommended to the trustees that James Cutler should be appointed dean of the new school. They agreed.

Creating a Professional School

Cutler began to organize the school in 1915, proposing that it offer graduate-level education consisting of academic coursework and supervised field work. He also proposed that it be named the School of Applied Social Sciences (SASS), to reflect the idea that social work practice is rooted in the academic discipline of sociology, rather than an extension of philanthropy or charity, which was the origin of other schools of social work.

The School's affiliation with the University and its strong association with social science positioned it at the cutting edge of a new profession still seeking legitimacy. That same year, Abraham Flexner, author of an earlier report on American medical education that revolutionized the teaching of physicians, came to the conclusion that social work was not, in fact, a profession itself, but rather a mediator between several helping professions. Flexner argued that social workers were employed in too many different areas—education, recreation, health, and welfare—to have a specific set of professional aims, and that there was not, as yet, a core curriculum for all social workers that involved learning a specific professional technique to be applied to situations in the field.

In Cutler's plans for SASS, the development of social work as a profession required a school with a strong basis in scientific method and research. Theoretical models taught in the classroom would be applied by students in their field placements, just as students in the hard sciences learned theory in the classroom and experimented by applying that theory in the laboratory. Research would be conducted by collecting data in the field, and

+ Visiting the Child Welfare Board.

analysis of the data would shape theoretical models to be taught in the future.

In December 1915, Cutler's plans were approved by the trustees and Western Reserve University President Charles Thwing. Cutler was formally appointed dean of the School of Applied Social Sciences at Western Reserve University—America's first university-affiliated professional graduate school of social work.

The First Class of Students

SASS enrolled its first 35 students, and classes began on September 19, 1916. There were 21 faculty members and tuition was $125 per year. Initially, the School had two divisions: Public Health Nursing, directed by Cecilia A. Evans of the University's nursing department, and Family Welfare and Social Service, directed by Jackson. Admissions, field placement, and financial support were initially tied directly to community agencies. On the one hand, this provided invaluable experience to students, who worked directly for an agency while taking coursework. It, however, also meant that the School was somewhat at the mercy of agency staffing and training needs, which constrained its ability to determine and deliver its curriculum without interference. It also conflicted with Dean Cutler's ambitions for the academic rigor of the program.

Dean, 1915–1941
JAMES E. CUTLER, PhD
Progressive Social Reformer and Longest-Serving Dean

After graduating with his bachelor's degree from the University of Colorado and a Doctorate in Sociology from Yale University, James Elbert Cutler was teaching at the University of Michigan and was a founding member of the American Sociological Society when Western Reserve University President Charles F. Thwing recruited him in 1907 to head the new Department of Sociology.

A scholar and progressive social reformer who saw research and teaching as tools to change society for the better, Cutler was an early and vocal advocate for the foundation of a university-affiliated professional school of social work at Western Reserve University. It was no surprise when he was tapped to help create the School of Applied Social Sciences and was appointed in 1915 to serve as its first dean.

His strong commitment to creating curricula that balanced social science methodology, community organization, and individual case work was coupled with a dedication to using Cleveland as a practical classroom—a visionary strategy that immediately put the School at the forefront of social work education.

After his appointment as dean, Cutler wrote *A Study in Professional Education at Western Reserve University: The School of Applied Social Sciences, 1916–1930* with Maurice Davie of Yale University, which outlined the School's first fifteen years, from its organization to its curriculum and community relationships. The book provided a model of university-based graduate-level social work education in what was still a fairly new field.

Cutler's scholarly writing also included the first book-length academic analysis of the history and causes of lynching in the United States, in which he strongly argued against the popular sentiment that mob violence was justified under certain circumstances. Published in 1905, *Lynch Law* continues to be cited in scholarship dealing with the history of violence against African Americans today.

Cutler was also the first president of the Cleveland Grand Jury Association, an organization concerned with public education about issues around law enforcement, criminal justice, and rehabilitation—a cause he took up with enthusiasm after his retirement as dean in 1941. Cutler was appointed Dean Emeritus in 1946 and died in 1959 at the age of 83.

+ Dean James E. Cutler.

The Great War and the First Graduates

World War I disrupted the School's early years, with staff and students contributing to the war effort. SASS provided training to American Red Cross workers and volunteers throughout the conflict. Several faculty members served in government during the war, including Dean Cutler, who worked in the Military Intelligence Division and the Morale Branch of the Chief of Staff Office in Washington, D.C., and Professor Raymond Moley, who worked as director of Cleveland's Americanization Board. In 1917, working with Cleveland's Division of Health and other private health agencies, the School took charge of one of Cleveland's health districts. Faculty worked out of the district office and students completed field work in the district.

The end of the decade saw the first graduates. Five students graduated in 1918 with the Certificate in Public Health Nursing. The following year produced the first two graduate students in social work: Future Dean Margaret H. Johnson, who was awarded a Master of Science with a designation

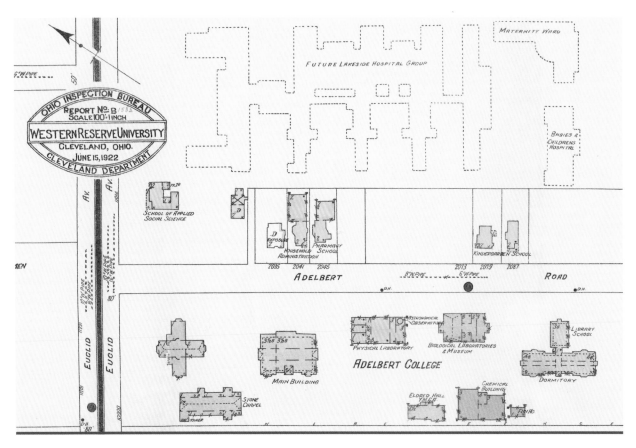

+ SASS is located at the corner of Euclid Avenue and Adelbert Road, June 1922.

in Social Administration, and Maude Madge McKinney, who was awarded a Master of Science with a designation in Public Administration, in 1919.

The Roaring Twenties

Throughout the 1920s, SASS continued to expand and add to its course offerings, beginning with the addition of a second year to the Social Administration program in the Master of Science.

The school grew rapidly throughout the decade, and relocated from the upper floor of Adelbert Hall to the Old Ford Residence (11014 Euclid Avenue) in 1921, where it would remain until the construction of the Allen Memorial Medical Library in 1925. The majority of students at this time—66 of the 100 full-time students—were enrolled in the public health nursing program, in large part because the American Red Cross provided support for nursing education in order to meet the need for nurses in rural areas. Demand from local social service agencies also fueled the School's growth, prompting the addition of a popular series of afternoon courses in family case work held in downtown Cleveland to accommodate the schedules of agency workers.

Innovative New Courses

In the 1921-22 Annual Report, Dean Cutler noted that the School's location in Cleveland allowed it

+ Old Ford House, home of SASS from 1921–1924.

FOUNDING FACULTY, 1916–1929

The individuals who established the first areas of study in the new School brought a wealth of experience from leadership roles in social welfare organizations and backgrounds in academic research, teaching, and publication. From the beginning, they sought to imbue their students with the intellectual and theoretical foundations of the social sciences and the practical skills necessary to serve the needs of a rapidly changing society. Members of this group went on to lead other social work schools, conduct groundbreaking research, and teach generations of social work professionals.

Mildred Chadsey, AB, PhB
   Associate Professor of Social Administration

James E. Cutler, PhD
   Dean of the School of Applied Social Sciences
   Professor of Sociology, Western Reserve University

Florence Day, AB, MSSA 1924
   Assistant Professor of Family Case Work

Cecilia A. Evans, RN
   Assistant Professor of Public Health Nursing
   Director, University Public Health Nursing District

Augustus Raymond Hatton, PhD
   Director, Division of Municipal Administration
   and Public Service
   Professor of Political Science, Western
   Reserve University

Marion G. Howell, RN, MSc
   Associate Professor of Public Health Nursing
   Director, University Public Health Nursing District

James F. Jackson, BS
   Superintendent, Cleveland Associated Charities
   Director, Division of Family Welfare and Social Service
   (later Social Administration)

Clara A. Kaiser, AB
   Director of Research, University Neighborhood Centers
   Assistant Professor of Group Work

Elizabeth P. Lyman
   Assistant Professor of Family Case Work

Maud Morlock, AB
   Assistant Professor of Child Welfare

Wilber I. Newstetter, AM
   Director, Woodland Center Settlement and University
   Neighborhood Centers

Agnes Schroeder, BS
   Assistant Professor of Medical Social Work

Anna Belle Tracy, AB
   Assistant Professor of Psychiatric Social Work

Helen M. Walker, AM
   Assistant Professor of Family Case Work

+ Florence Day, ca. 1923–24
(Western Reserve Historical Society).

+ Elizabeth Lyman, 1920
(Western Reserve Historical Society).

+ Helen Walker, ca. 1923–24
(Western Reserve Historical Society).

a unique opportunity for professional social work training, as the city was "a better equipped field for training work than most other colleges and universities can offer."

Throughout the decade, the School created several new courses of study:

- Child Welfare was launched in 1921-22 and led by Maud Morlock, a graduate of Chicago's School of Civics and Philanthropy. The course began with 22 students, all employees of the Cleveland Humane Society or Children's Bureau.
- The School also expanded its training course in family case work to a second year, with field work taking place under the auspices of Associated Charities.
- In 1923, SASS offered the first university training course in group social work in the United States, taught by director Mildred Chadsey.
- In 1925, the school expanded its field placements with support of the Commonwealth Fund to include the Child Guidance Clinic. It conducted its first summer camp training institute for students in the group service program, held at a YWCA camp in Madison, Ohio.

Financial Turmoil

Despite the growth of its programs and continuing demand for trained social workers, the School had trouble securing funding during the 1920s. In 1923, it was able to cover its budget deficit with $7,500 from the Community Fund, even though the Fund cautioned Western Reserve University that funding the School was its responsibility. In 1924, University President Robert E. Vinson asked Sydnor Walker, a director of the Laura Spelman Rockefeller Foundation of New York and an expert on the field of social work education, to travel to Cleveland to evaluate the School's programs. Walker reported her findings in May 1925. She noted that SASS appeared to be too financially tied to the agencies to which it provided training and recommended that

+ Maud Morlock, 1929.

+ Mildred Chadsey, ca. 1920s.

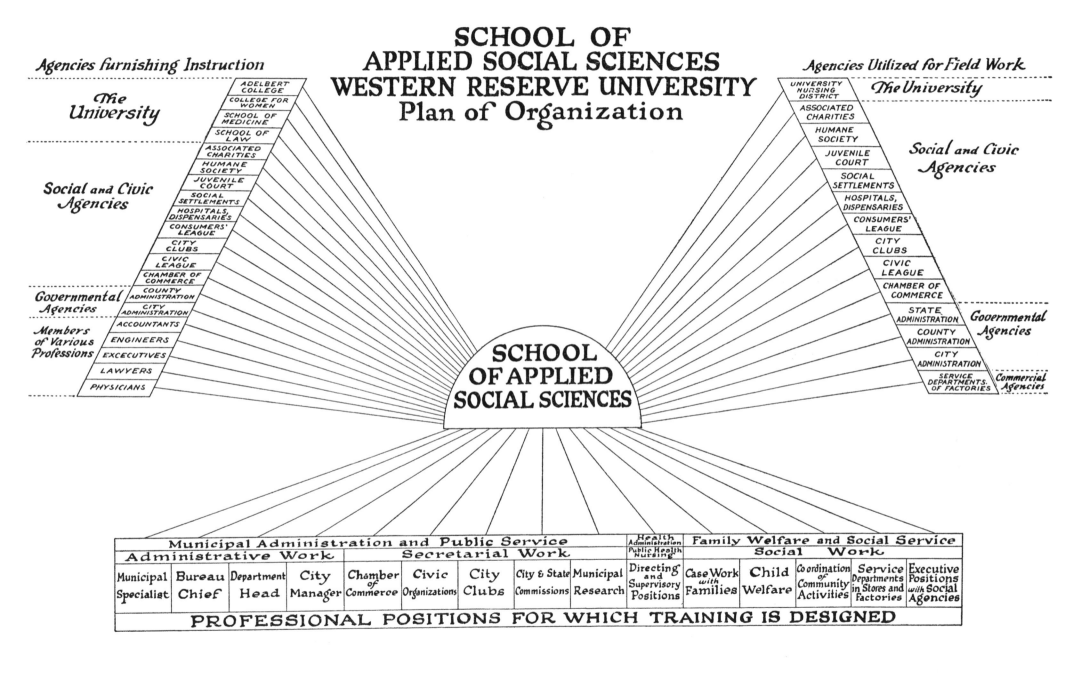

SCHOOL OF
APPLIED SOCIAL SCIENCES
WESTERN RESERVE UNIVERSITY
Plan of Organization

Agencies furnishing Instruction

The University

Social and Civic Agencies

Governmental Agencies

Members of Various Professions

ADELBERT COLLEGE
COLLEGE FOR WOMEN
SCHOOL OF MEDICINE
SCHOOL OF LAW
ASSOCIATED CHARITIES
HUMANE SOCIETY
JUVENILE COURT
SOCIAL SETTLEMENTS
HOSPITALS, DISPENSARIES
CONSUMERS' LEAGUE
CITY CLUBS
CIVIC LEAGUE
CHAMBER OF COMMERCE
COUNTY ADMINISTRATION
CITY ADMINISTRATION
ACCOUNTANTS
ENGINEERS
EXECUTIVES
LAWYERS
PHYSICIANS

SCHOOL OF APPLIED SOCIAL SCIENCES

Agencies Utilized for Field Work

The University

Social and Civic Agencies

Governmental Agencies

Commercial Agencies

UNIVERSITY NURSING DISTRICT
ASSOCIATED CHARITIES
HUMANE SOCIETY
JUVENILE COURT
SOCIAL SETTLEMENTS
HOSPITALS, DISPENSARIES
CONSUMERS' LEAGUE
CITY CLUBS
CIVIC LEAGUE
CHAMBER OF COMMERCE
STATE ADMINISTRATION
COUNTY ADMINISTRATION
CITY ADMINISTRATION
SERVICE DEPARTMENTS OF FACTORIES

Municipal Administration and Public Service							Health Administration / Public Health Nursing	Family Welfare and Social Service					
Administrative Work				Secretarial Work				Social Work					
Municipal Specialist	Bureau Chief	Department Head	City Manager	Chamber of Commerce	Civic Organizations	City Clubs	City & State Commissions	Municipal Research	Directing and Supervisory Positions	Case Work with Families	Child Welfare	Coordination of Community Activities	Service Departments in Stores and Factories	Executive Positions with Social Agencies

PROFESSIONAL POSITIONS FOR WHICH TRAINING IS DESIGNED

+ Plan of Organization in the 1925-26 Course Bulletin.

UNIVERSITY NEIGHBORHOOD CENTERS:
America's First University-Sponsored Social Group Work Laboratory

Founded in 1926, University Neighborhood Centers (later known as University Settlement) provided students with intensive field placement experiences and the opportunity to participate in front line sociological research. Students lived in four different houses located around the South Broadway area of Cleveland and worked with community members and organizations to identify and meet their needs with recreational, educational, and economically beneficial activities.

The initiative was spearheaded by Wilber I. Newstetter, AM, a native Ohioan and former master's student of Dean Cutler. Joel B. Hayden, Pastor of Fairmount Presbyterian Church and a local progressive reformer, helped the School secure funding for the pioneering venture from the Laura Spellman Rockefeller Memorial Foundation.

Generous funding was also provided by local philanthropist and heiress to the Standard Oil fortune, Elizabeth Bingham Blossom, who gave $360,000 (approximately $6.3 million in 2017 dollars) to support the centers between their inception in 1926 until 1941, when the Cleveland Welfare Federation took over operations.

In the fifteen years the University Neighborhood Centers were under the auspices of the School, they trained more than 100 students in the Group Work concentration and provided invaluable data for research and publications, including Grace Longwell Coyle's highly influential book, *Studies in Group Behavior.*

the School be placed on an independent financial footing to become less dependent on agency staffing requirements.

Based on Walker's report, the University's Board of Trustees approved a resolution in June 1925 stating that SASS was responsible for covering its annual budget deficit. Realizing that the School was in danger of shutting down, Dean Cutler solicited letters of support from prominent Clevelanders and members of the national social work community, including Jane Addams of Chicago's Hull House. In November, the faculty presented a report to the trustees about the School's educational policies and its importance to the community, recommending additional coursework in medical, psychiatric, and school social work, as well as, adding research requirements for students. They also recommended developing case work classes for employees of social work agencies that dealt with juvenile delinquency. Still, the resolution remained in place.

In early 1926, a group of students joined with Reverend Joel B. Hayden of Fairmount Presbyterian Church and Wilber I. Newstetter, director of the Woodland Center settlement house, to advocate for the creation of a group work training center, in response to the need for social welfare assistance among the Polish and Slovenian neighborhoods in southeast

+ Rev. Joel B. Hayden, 1935 *(Western Reserve Historical Society).*

+ The five houses on Adelbert Road that SASS occupied from 1924 to 1951, earning it the nickname "School of Little Houses."

ALUMNI PROFILE
Ella Mae Cheeks Johnson, MSSA 1928

The author of the autobiography, *It Is Well with My Soul: The Extraordinary Life of a 106-Year-Old Woman*, Ella Mae Cheeks Johnson enrolled in the School of Applied Social Sciences in 1926 after graduating from Fisk University, a popular recruitment partner for the School to this day.

As a student, her field placement was at Associated Charities, and she had fond memories of her field instruc-

+ Ella Mae Cheeks Johnson's memoir *(Penguin Books)*.

tor, Helen Walker. She graduated in 1928, then worked for Cuyahoga County for Aid to Families with Dependent Children (AFDC) and the Child Welfare Board.

Among Johnson's clients was Louise C. Stokes, whose sons were future Congressman Louis Stokes and his brother Carl, the first African-American mayor of Cleveland. Well into his 80s, Congressman Stokes warmly recalled Johnson and her visits to his home, as well as her kindness to him and his mother.

Upon her retirement from social work, Johnson traveled to 30 countries and volunteered for the Mount Zion Congregational Church, Alpha Kappa Alpha, and the Phillis Wheatley Association. She maintained her concern for social causes, fundraising for HIV/AIDS victims and the charity Smile Train. In 2009, at the age of 105, she attended President Barack Obama's inauguration.

When Johnson died in March 2010, her autobiography had been recently published, and she was the oldest living African-American graduate of Case Western Reserve University. Her papers are archived at the Western Reserve Historical Society and available to researchers.

Cleveland. The School joined with a newly-created citizen advisory committee to seek funding for the new center from the Welfare Federation, the Community Chest, and the Laura Spellman Rockefeller Memorial Foundation. They were told, however, that the trustees' resolution regarding the School's budget deficits was a barrier to fundraising. The advisory committee petitioned the trustees to rescind their resolution, which they did in May, allowing SASS to gain foundation support for the new center. The Board of Trustees also passed a new resolution in support of the School and voted to assume its budget deficit for 1926.

With the establishment of University Neighborhood Centers (later known as University Settlement) under Newstetter's direction, SASS now had a strong group service work program that was entirely under its control. In 1929, the course would be renamed the Group Work Program, following national social work trends. By the end of the decade, Clara Kaiser joined the staff as Director of Research, and Newstetter established the Wawokiye Camp Experiment, which provided a camping experience for troubled young men, as well as a site for group work research for students (see Chapter 2).

"School of Little Houses"

SASS continued to expand throughout the late 1920s, assisted by a five-year matching grant from the Rockefeller Foundation. The School hired more faculty and administrative staff, including three secretaries, a registrar, a librarian, and, notably, executive secretary and future Dean Margaret H. Johnson (one of the first alumni). SASS expanded on campus as well, with offices and classrooms in what became known as the "five little houses" on Adelbert Road.

In 1927, Agnes Schroeder, who was in the social service department at Lakeside Hospital, was asked to establish a course in medical social work. A year later, with support from the Commonwealth Fund, the School added a specialization in psychiatric course work under director Anna Belle Tracy, executive secretary of the Cleveland Home Service Section of the American Red Cross.

By decade's end, there continued to be great demand for social workers, particularly after the stock market crash in October 1929 increased the number of people needing aid. The School of Applied Social Sciences was firmly established and ready to meet the needs of those affected by the Great Depression. +

+ Agnes Schroeder, 1920 *(Western Reserve Historical Society)*.

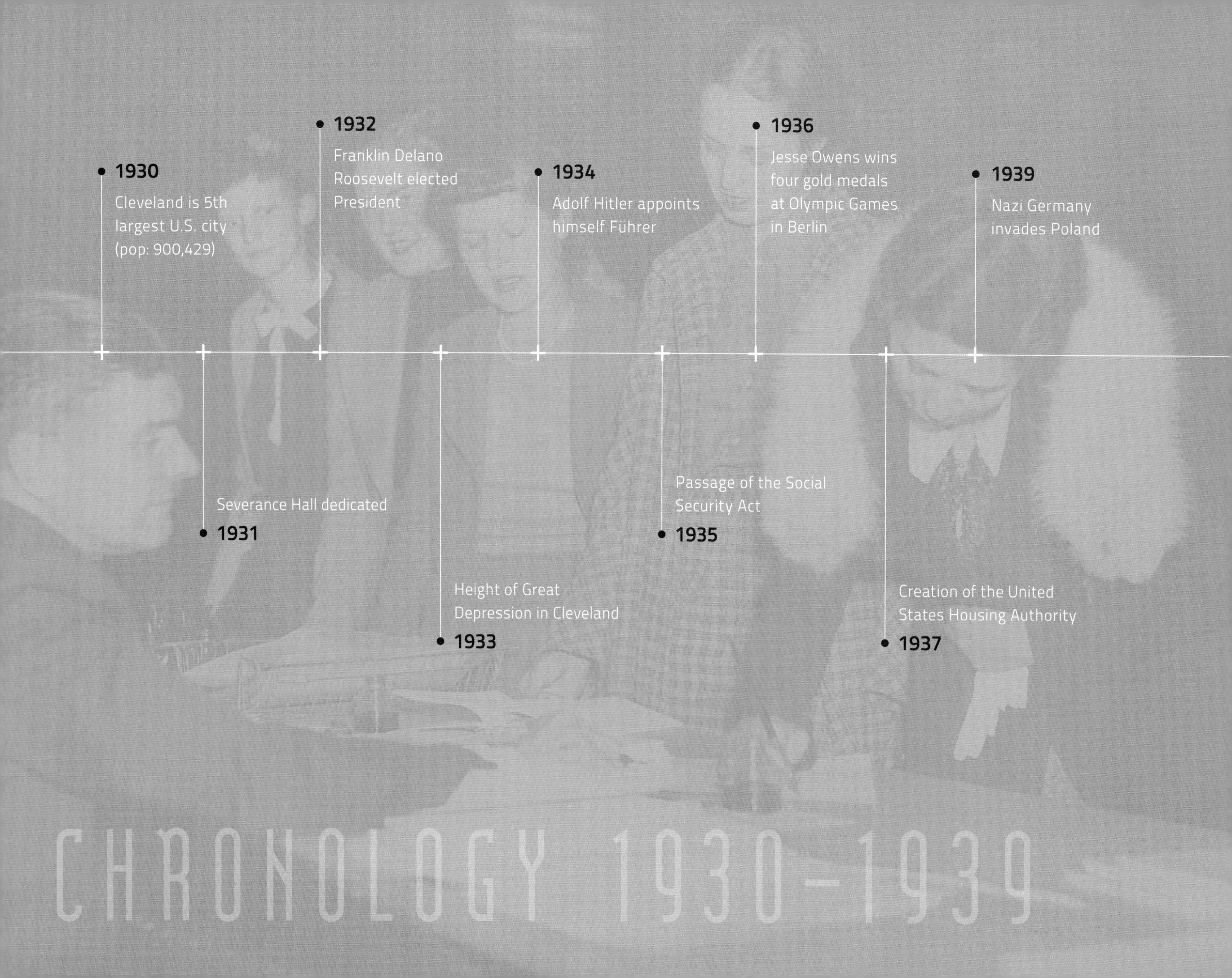

1930

Cleveland is 5th
largest U.S. city
(pop: 900,429)

1932

Franklin Delano
Roosevelt elected
President

1934

Adolf Hitler appoints
himself Führer

1936

Jesse Owens wins
four gold medals
at Olympic Games
in Berlin

1939

Nazi Germany
invades Poland

Severance Hall dedicated

1931

Passage of the Social
Security Act

1935

Height of Great
Depression in Cleveland

1933

Creation of the United
States Housing Authority

1937

CHRONOLOGY 1930-1939

CHAPTER 2

Coming of Age

In the midst of the Great Depression, public and private social welfare agencies struggled to hire qualified applicants to help in every area of human services: public health, administration of financial relief, child welfare, mental health, school social work, and group work. The School of Applied Social Sciences could not train students fast enough to meet demand. As one reporter quipped in 1930, "So far as I know, there is no unemployment in social work in Cleveland."

A National Emergency

To give some sense of the economic need of families in the city in 1930, the Cleveland Parks Department provided an opportunity for male heads of household who wanted short term work. In just two days in October, 6,500 men signed up. By November, when the opportunity was offered again, 11,200 men applied in a single day. This locally run and financed program provided 12 days of work and $57.60 of income for each participant. It didn't make a dent in the surging unemployment and ensuing poverty throughout the city. By 1933, approximately 50% of industrial workers in Cleveland were unemployed. In December of 1935, 38% of families in Cleveland and 30% of families in Cuyahoga County were on relief.

Until federal dollars became available in 1935, all relief in the city and county came from local and state dollars distributed primarily by private agencies, most importantly by Associated Charities and the Jewish Social Service Bureau, where students had field placements. When the Cuyahoga County Relief Administration was formed to coordinate the community response in August of 1933, it was created by taking over 1,300 Associated Charities staff members in twelve district offices and a smaller number of employees of the Jewish Social Service Bureau, which had already been providing relief to 40,000 families. Similarly, when the Cuyahoga County Child Welfare Board was created in 1930 to deal with the overwhelming number of children in need of shelter, they also began by co-opting the employees of the Humane Society and the Welfare Association for Jewish Children, agencies which were already placing children in foster homes and orphanages.

Surging Enrollment and a New Assistant Dean

As these agencies struggled to meet urgent community needs, they sought more trained workers

+ Field clinic in the University Public Health Nursing District, January 1937.

to serve as administrators of these newly-public programs. Suddenly, SASS graduates and current students were much more likely to be supervisors to untrained case workers than to be working directly with clients. In this national emergency, the School attracted students from across the region and nation. By 1934, 265 were enrolled in the Master's program, specializing in family case work, public health nursing, and group work. Dean Cutler continued to split his time between SASS and Western Reserve University's sociology department and, in order to address the demands of increasing numbers of students, Margaret H. Johnson, MSSA 1919, was promoted from Executive Secretary to Assistant Dean.

One of the first recipients of a graduate degree from SASS, Johnson was also a group work instructor and was instrumental in the founding of the School's Alumni Association, which was a major contributor to the funding of student scholarships and later the construction of Beaumont Hall. Johnson was known for her student-centered approach and continuing relationships with alumni. Together, Dean Cutler and Assistant Dean Johnson's experience and active management guided the School through what was to be a turbulent decade.

Cleveland's social service agencies made "herculean efforts ... to maintain service in the face of

ALUMNI PROFILE:
Henry L. Zucker, MSSA 1935

Henry L. Zucker's impulse to serve the community became his vocation. A native Clevelander, he graduated from Glenville High School and Adelbert College of Western Reserve University. As an undergraduate, he volunteered at the Jewish Service Bureau, which was working directly to assist low income immigrant Jewish families struggling with employment, health, housing, and education.

Upon graduation from SASS in 1935, he went to work for the Cuyahoga County Relief Administration, which was in charge of distributing financial and social welfare support to families during the Great Depression. He ultimately became its chief executive.

In the late 1930s, Zucker was a leader of the Welfare Federation in Cleveland, which conducted the yearly Community Chest fundraising campaign and distributed proceeds to community agencies—what later became known as United Way Services of Cleveland. After a decade of service to the Welfare Federation, he became Associate Director of the Jewish Community Federation, then rising to the position of Executive Director (1948-1965), then Executive Vice President (1965-1975).

In the aftermath of World War II, Zucker was a consultant to the Jewish Joint Distribution Committee, helping to reestablish Jewish communities across Europe, and assisting the resettlement of war refugees in the newly created state of Israel. In his work for the Jewish Community Federation, Zucker helped to create an endowment model in Cleveland that was replicated across the country. He also remained close to the School, chairing the Convocation Committee for the 50th Anniversary and serving on the Dean's Council and Visiting Committee.

After his retirement from the Jewish Community Federation, Zucker became Director of the Premier Industrial Philanthropic Program, now the Jack, Joseph and Morton Mandel Foundation. Zucker and Morton L. Mandel were seminal in the creation of the Mandel Center for Nonprofit Organizations in 1984 at Case Western Reserve University.

"Henry Zucker had a combination of a very clear mind and a warm Jewish heart. He understood how to help people grow," said Mandel, who led Zucker's colleagues and friends in the creation of an endowed professorship in Zucker's honor in 1985, to celebrate the 50th anniversary of his graduation from SASS and his 75th birthday. Today, David Biegel, PhD, is the Henry L. Zucker Professor in Social Work Practice.

+ Henry L. Zucker, MSSA 1935.

falling income" and exponentially increasing case-loads. As a result, agencies began to hire more untrained social work "aides." Second year students found themselves supervising aides in their fieldwork placements. Often, aides were college graduates without social work backgrounds who came to resent that, regardless of their experience, promotion within agencies went almost exclusively to those with social work degrees. A 1938 publication explained that "Cleveland is one of many cities which seeks to maintain a high standard among its social workers. In certain agencies it is possible to secure employment as an 'aide' without the educational background. However, there is a difference in the scale of salaries paid to trained social workers and aides, just as there is a difference in the wages of trained nurses and practical nurses."

Western Reserve University and SASS were not immune to the effects of the financial crisis. Faculty faced 30% pay cuts and layoffs. They struggled to provide the fundamentals of social work training to the increasing number of students pouring in. Like the rest of the country, the School was forced to do more with fewer resources. At the same time, from the perspective of recent graduates, the School had failed to prepare them for the new administrative responsibilities they now faced. By 1935, SASS began to offer courses

+ Students register for classes in 1937 at Cleveland College, a joint venture between Western Reserve University and the Case School of Applied Science for adult learners where SASS faculty taught classes in social work.

addressing some of these supervisory responsibilities and incorporating the new realities of public and private cooperation in the provision of social services. These new courses had titles like "Public Social Work in a Case Work Agency" and "The State and Social Work."

As the scope of work in the field expanded with the establishment of federal programs, the School revised its curriculum. Medical social work and family casework became two-year concentrations. Courses in family casework ceased to be located at Associated Charities offices and were moved to campus. Field work placements expanded to include the Jewish Social Service and the Cleveland chapter of the American Red Cross, with which the School had been cooperating since World War I.

+ Field clinic in the University Public Health Nursing District, January 1937.

Alumni Speak Up

By 1936, alumni had become dissatisfied with the School's perceived political neutrality in approaching the problems of the Great Depression. Students, faculty, and alumni were facing a greater amount of desperation among their clients. Even in placements with recreational purposes, like organizing playground activities or scouting, children and youth were experiencing the effects of their families' profound struggles with unemployment, homelessness, and illness. Alumni met in a series of roundtable discussions that resulted in a critical report of the School's faculty and administration. Alumni argued that their education should have had a deeper foundation in research and prepared them for public advocacy and policy reform as well as work with individuals and families. Faculty were generally receptive to the first two issues, but were wary of taking a public position on the role of social workers and social welfare agencies in public policy debates.

One alumnus argued: "We who have been face-to-face with problems confronting social work today have been struck by the dual role of social work: that of 'adjustments individual by individual between man and his social environment' and that of adjusting a hopelessly maladjusted social environment to meet the needs of large masses of individuals." Dean Cutler and other faculty held the opposing view that "The role of the militant reformer and agitator is not a formula for a profession.... The detached viewpoint gives balance, poise and judgment." On a more practical level, community agencies were cognizant that, given their limited resources, any focus on advocacy would reduce the available staff time and energy to address immediate client needs.

In 1934, Grace Longwell Coyle joined the School's faculty when she was appointed Director of Research at the University Neighborhood Centers. The relationship between the School and the University Neighborhood Centers changed in 1936 upon its incorporation and merger with the Welfare Federation, when it was renamed University Settlement. The School would continue its relationship with University Settlement through the early 1940s, but it no longer served as a research laboratory for the program in group work.

Dean Cutler, who until this point was serving both as a faculty member in Western Reserve's sociology department and as Dean, became the full-time Dean of the School in 1936. During the late 1930s, enrollment decreased, despite increases in enrollment in social work schools nationally.

One of the factors at play was the cumbersome process of admission, which required students to be admitted both by the faculty in an area of specialization and by a specific field placement agency. Attempts to centralize admissions were thwarted by community agencies, which feared they might miss out on the best students for field placements and thus have a less desirable pool of potential employees upon graduation.

Time for Change

The close relationship between field placement agencies and the School had been an asset twenty years earlier, but the hurdles to admission and the financial relationship between agencies and the School needed reworking. Faculty were overworked and frustrated. University trustees questioned a tuition structure in which agencies paid tuition for student staff members, rather than students paying the School directly. SASS was struggling under a multi-year deficit, and the University pressured Dean Cutler to make substantive changes. With the assistance of the Welfare Federation and local agencies, the School embarked on a study of its educational programs,

+ SASS students conducting fieldwork at the University Neighborhood Centers, 1936-37. Standing, left to right: Mary Emma King, Marjorie Buckholz, Dorothy Smith, Robert Morrison, Esther Test, Wilbur A. Joseph, Mildred Creighton, Dean Longfellow, Elizabeth Tracy. Sitting, left to right: Robert Archer, Virginia Goodwin, Martha Noell, Mary Eleen Finley, Irene Beadle, Margaret Johnson, Christine Rayer, Arthur Davis *(Western Reserve Historical Society)*.

TUITION AND FEES, 1930–31

- Tuition: $300 per year
- Camp Institute Fee (group work students only): $7.50
- Graduate Fee: $10
- Student Health Service Fee: $5.00
- Transcript Fee: $1.00
- Estimated cost of textbooks and supplies: $15

with the goal of aligning them with the trends in the changing field of social work in the United States, and hopefully solving their budget woes in the process.

In October 1938, SASS hired prominent Philadelphia social worker Dorothy Kahn to supervise the committees conducting a curricular study. In December, she presented a comprehensive report to the School. Kahn recommended:

- SASS centralize its administration—including streamlining admissions and providing scholarship funds through the School rather than individual field agencies.
- Create a standard core curriculum for students with options for course specializations in their second year rather than tailoring course work to fit the needs of the specific local agencies with which students were paired.
- Expand field placement opportunities so that students would be able to experience work in multiple agencies.
- Recruit faculty from graduate programs outside of Western Reserve University. Hiring faculty with national reputations would invigorate the community work being done in Cleveland and attract more ambitious students.
- Faculty should focus on teaching and academic research and balance their contribu-

GRACE LONGWELL COYLE, PhD
NASW Social Work Pioneer
Trailblazing Innovator of Group Work

Grace Longwell Coyle is considered one of the most influential people in the history of social work. Widely considered the founder of group work, Coyle's contributions to the field have been compared to the foundational work of Mary Richmond and Jane Addams.

Born in 1892 in North Adams, Massachusetts, Coyle earned a bachelor's degree from Wellesley College in 1914, a certificate from the New York School of Philanthropy in 1915,

+ Grace Longwell Coyle in 1956.

and a master's degree in economics (1928) and doctorate in sociology from Columbia University (1931).

Early in her career, Coyle worked in settlement houses and the YWCA, where she developed adult education and recreation programs. In 1923, she developed the first group work training course for SASS.

Coyle's doctoral dissertation, *Social Progress in Organized Groups* (1930), reflected her interest in group dynamics. In 1930, she directed research and organized institutes as head of the YWCA national laboratory division. SASS hired Coyle in 1934 as an Assistant Professor. She was promoted to Associate Professor in 1936 and Professor three years later. In 1938, Coyle was appointed Director of Group Work.

Coyle's research was a major contribution to the acceptance of group work as part of social work practice, and she advocated for the integration of group work with case work. Her publications include her landmark book *Studies in Group Behavior* (1937), as well as *Group Experiences and Democratic Values* (1947), *Group Work with American Youth* (1948), and *Social Science in the Professional Education of Social Workers* (1958).

Coyle remained active with the YWCA and served as President of the National Conference of Social Work in 1940, the American Association of Social Workers in 1942, and the Council on Social Work Education in 1958.

Coyle taught at the School until she died in 1962 at the age of 69. In 1965, SASS created its first endowed chair in her honor. It is currently held by Elizabeth M. Tracy, PhD, the Grace Longwell Coyle Professor in Social Work.

WAWOKIYE CAMP:
A Group Work Experiment in the Woods

Founded in 1926 as an overnight camp for troubled boys ages 8-17, Wawokiye Camp was also an experiment in group dynamics led by faculty members Wilber I. Newstetter and Marc J. Feldstein. It provided the ideal opportunity to observe group dynamics over time in a controlled environment and led to two influential research publications.

Boys in groups of thirty attended the camp in five-week sessions, removed from the influences of school, family, and pre-existing peer groups. Newstetter, Feldstein, and a team of students attempted to track the boys' ability to adjust socially to their new circumstances, developing tools to measure the "group acceptance of the individual" and the "individual's acceptance of the group."

Wawokiye Camp was a collaboration between the School and the Cleveland Child Guidance Clinic, which referred the boys and provided two on-site psychiatrists. Other boys were referred through University Neighborhood Centers. Located on several acres of woodland in Willoughby, Ohio, with direct access to Lake Erie, it offered normal camp activities including "hiking, fishing, archery, swimming, canoeing, baseball, camp craft, handcraft and games," but also gave boys a great deal of freedom to determine whether they would participate and what activities each tent group would pursue.

The experiment led to the publication in 1930 of *Wawokiye Camp: A Research Project in Group Work* by Newstetter and Feldstein. In 1938, Newstetter, Feldstein, and Theodore M. Newcomb published a book-length sociometric study, *Group Adjustment: A Study in Experimental Sociology*, based on further research conducted at the Wawokiye Camp during more than ten summers. Both works helped create a new standard for sociometric methodology that influenced social science research for decades.

tions to local agencies, noting that in certain situations "faculty members seem to be in danger of being used as auxiliary staff rather than colleagues or professional counselors."

- Finally, she urged University trustees to consider construction of a modern building to house the School.

SASS began to implement many of these changes, among which was the relocation of the public health nursing division to the Frances Payne Bolton School of Nursing at Western Reserve University. The changes, however, didn't come fast enough. In 1939, SASS was struggling under a cumulative deficit of $60,000 and projected an additional $30,000 deficit by the end of 1940.

Shaping Social Work

Remarkably, throughout the decade, the School distinguished itself through major publications that went on to shape new fields of study in social work. While alumni may not have felt their education included enough research, faculty were deeply engaged in groundbreaking studies that went on to shape their respective fields.

In 1930, Wilber I. Newstetter and Marc J. Feldstein published *Wawokiye Camp: A Research Project in Group Work*, which detailed their work with the Wawokiye Camp experiment with troubled boys.

+ Aerial view of Wawokiye Camp by A. Pryber on July 24, 1932 *(Western Reserve Historical Society).*

That same year, Dean Cutler and Maurice Rea Davie, a former Western Reserve University sociology professor who taught at Yale University, published *A Study in Professional Education at Western Reserve University: The School of Applied Social Sciences, 1916-1930*, describing the work of the School in great detail. Dean Cutler and Professor Davie sought to share the curricular approach of the school, which emphasized a balance between academic coursework, field work in community agencies, and research. As one of the first university-affiliated social work schools, SASS's journey served as a guide for administrators of other schools of social work seeking insight into the processes of social work education.

In 1937, Grace Longwell Coyle edited and published her influential book *Studies in Group Behavior*, based upon group work records written by SASS students working at the University Neighborhood Centers (later University Settlement). It was reviewed by every major social work journal and went on to become a seminal text in the field of group work. *Social Service Review* compared its influence on group work with that of Mary Richmond's revolutionary book *Social Diagnosis*, which established case work methods that became foundational in the field. In 1938, Coyle succeeded Newstetter as Director of Group Work at SASS. They are often credited with creating modern group work, and they advocated for the specialization throughout their careers.

The School of Applied Social Sciences was integral to the functioning of many social welfare agencies in Cleveland during the Great Depression. Its students and faculty viewed the city as their laboratory—a place where theory and practice came together to build a stronger community—and as their responsibility to serve others. ✦

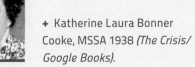

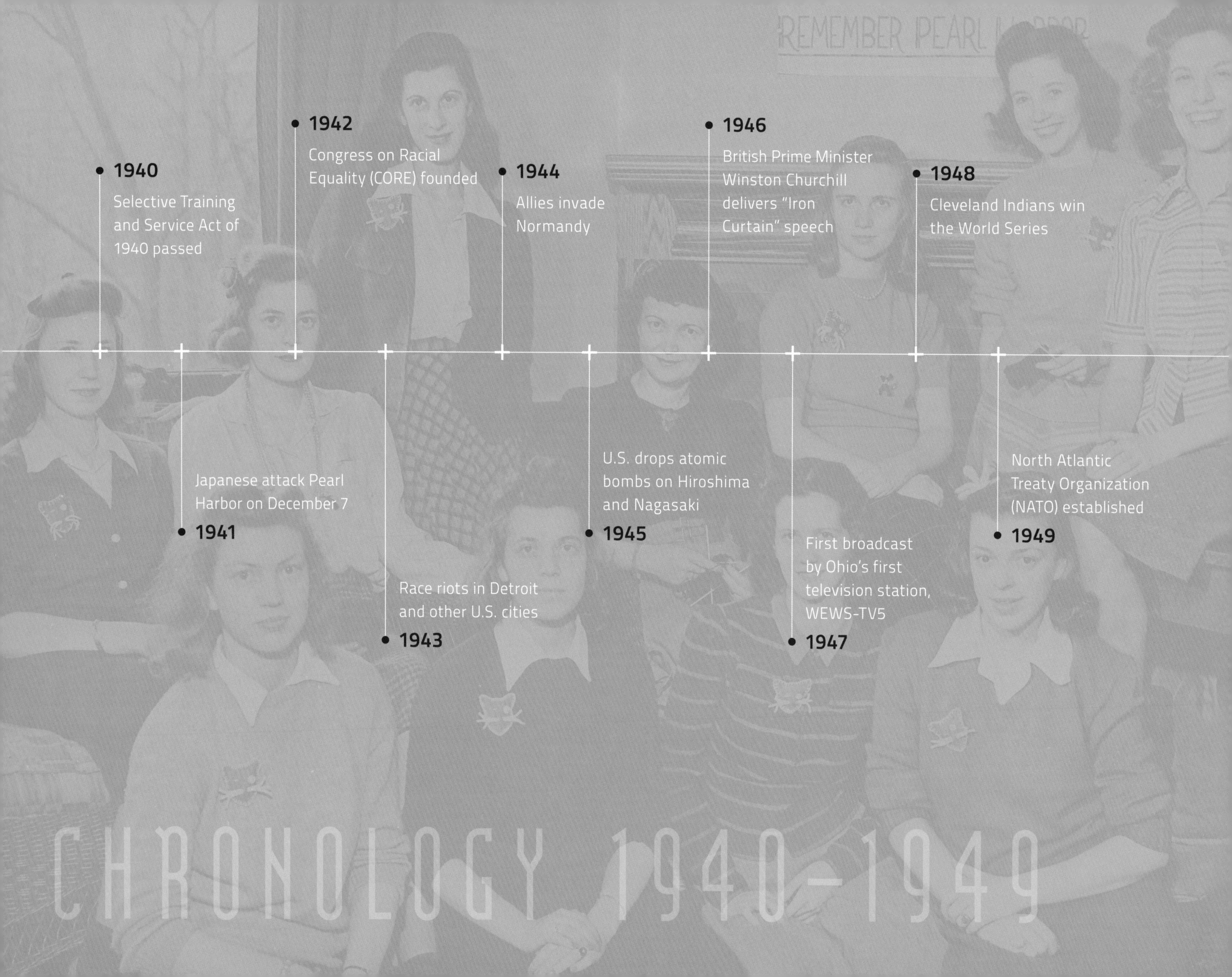

1940

Selective Training and Service Act of 1940 passed

1942

Congress on Racial Equality (CORE) founded

1944

Allies invade Normandy

1946

British Prime Minister Winston Churchill delivers "Iron Curtain" speech

1948

Cleveland Indians win the World Series

Japanese attack Pearl Harbor on December 7

1941

U.S. drops atomic bombs on Hiroshima and Nagasaki

1945

North Atlantic Treaty Organization (NATO) established

1949

Race riots in Detroit and other U.S. cities

1943

First broadcast by Ohio's first television station, WEWS-TV5

1947

CHRONOLOGY 1940–1949

CHAPTER 3

A Call to Service

In 1915, Dean James Cutler's goals in founding the School of Applied Social Sciences were to establish social work as a legitimate profession, the School as a leading program in graduate social work education, and SASS as an integral part of Western Reserve University and the greater community. In all of these areas, his tenure had been a success. In the 1941 annual report, Assistant Dean Margaret Johnson wrote that SASS was the third largest school of social work in the United States, based on the number of full time students pursuing a graduate degree. Under Cutler, the School had "grown to a position of national and international recognition as evidenced by its alumni who are now holding responsible positions in every State and in many foreign countries."

While the profession had matured and SASS's reputation had been established, the School's financial relationship to community agencies had started to become limiting. Admissions and School finances were complicated by the agencies' control over student selection and provision of tuition dollars. As a result, the School had little flexibility in allocating its own finances, and it was running a significant deficit by the end of the 1930s. In June 1940, the Western Reserve University Board of Trustees passed a resolution stating that if the School of Applied Social Sciences could not come up with a clear plan to address its financial problems by spring, "the School shall be discontinued at that time."

Time for New Leadership

A fresh perspective and new leadership were needed. Dean Cutler, who was struggling with health issues, decided to retire in order to make room for a new administrator with the energy and experience to stabilize the financial situation and preserve the School's future. In the interim, Assistant Dean Johnson took on the responsibility of Acting Dean. After an extensive search, Leonard W. Mayo was recruited to become the second dean of SASS, tasked with bringing the school into its next chapter.

A faculty member at the New York School of Social Work at Columbia University, Dean Mayo had spent eight years as an administrator of children's institutions, and he brought a knack for fundraising and public relations with him to SASS. He immediately reached out to foundations on the East Coast that were known for their investments in social work education and began a personal

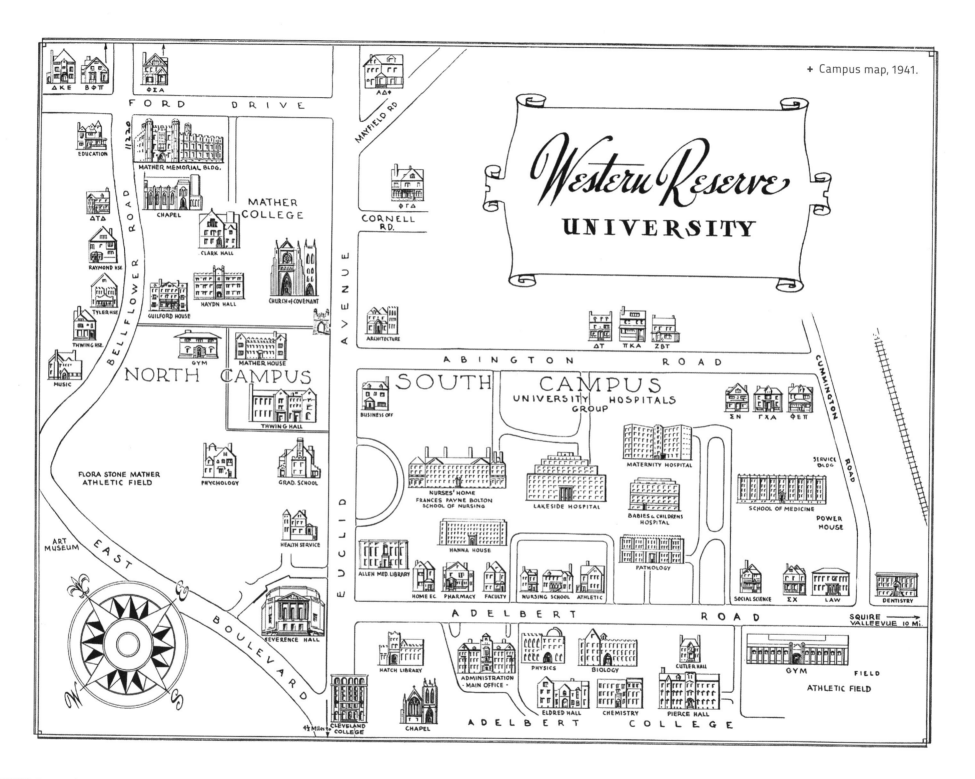

ΔΚΕ   ΒΦΠ

ΦΣΔ

ΛΔΦ

FORD   DRIVE

MAYFIELD RD

EDUCATION

11220

MATHER MEMORIAL BLDG.

ΔΤΔ

CHAPEL

MATHER
COLLEGE

ΦΓΔ

CORNELL
RD.

RAYMOND HSE.

CLARK HALL

CHURCH of COVENANT

AVENUE

TYLER HSE.

HAYDN HALL

GUILFORD HOUSE

THWING HSE.

MUSIC

GYM

MATHER HOUSE

NORTH   CAMPUS

SOUTH   CAMPUS

ARCHITECTURE

ΔΤ   ΠΚΑ   ΖΒΤ

ABINGTON   ROAD

THWING HALL

BUSINESS OFF

UNIVERSITY HOSPITALS
GROUP

ΣΝ ΓΧΑ ΦΕΠ

CUMMINGTON   ROAD

FLORA STONE MATHER
ATHLETIC FIELD

PHYCHOLOGY

GRAD. SCHOOL

MATERNITY HOSPITAL

SERVICE
BLDG

NURSES' HOME
FRANCES PAYNE BOLTON
SCHOOL OF NURSING

LAKESIDE HOSPITAL

BABIES & CHILDRENS
HOSPITAL

SCHOOL OF MEDICINE

POWER
HOUSE

ART
MUSEUM

HEALTH SERVICE

EUCLID

HANNA HOUSE

ALLEN MED. LIBRARY

PATHOLOGY

SOCIAL SCIENCE

ΣΧ   LAW

DENTISTRY

EAST

HOME EC. PHARMACY FACULTY

NURSING SCHOOL ATHLETIC

SEVERENCE HALL

BOULEVARD

ADELBERT   ROAD

SQUIRE
VALLEEVUE 10 Mi.

HATCH LIBRARY

ADMINISTRATION
· MAIN OFFICE ·

PHYSICS

BIOLOGY

CUTLER HALL

GYM   FIELD

ATHLETIC FIELD

4½ Miles to
CLEVELAND
COLLEGE

CHAPEL

ELDRED HALL   CHEMISTRY   PIERCE HALL

ADELBERT   COLLEGE

S   E   W   N

campaign to meet with philanthropic individuals and corporations in Cleveland to share the important work the School was doing. By June 1941, he had assuaged the financial fears of the university trustees, in the process forging a new and more collegial relationship with President Winfred G. Leutner and the university community at large.

Dean Mayo set out to modernize and simplify the School's internal administration, implementing many of the recommendations of Dorothy Kahn's report. He made faculty decision-making more democratic, streamlined admissions, expanded the number of agencies that accepted students for field work placements, and made it possible for students to gain exposure to multiple organizations in their two years of school, rather than being locked in to one agency from beginning to end. The modernization of policies and procedures for field placements and the clarification of thesis requirements directly impacted students and improved their experience at the School.

Beginning in 1941 and with the cooperation of the faculty, Dean Mayo worked to "determine what subject matter is common to all of social work and hence what subject matter and courses should be required of all students." Their solution was ultimately to focus on theory and method in the first year of the program, and practical application in the second year. This model enabled students

Dean, 1941–1948
LEONARD W. MAYO
A Passion for Child and Social Welfare

Born in 1899, Leonard W. Mayo grew up at the Berkshire Industrial Farm, a working farm for wayward boys where his father was the director and where his interest in child welfare began.

After graduating from Colby College in Maine, Mayo worked at three different residential facilities for boys until he returned to school to earn his master's degree from the New York School of Social Work at Columbia University,

+ Dean Leonard W. Mayo.

where he later taught. He arrived at SASS with deep experience in social welfare administration, having served as the Assistant Director of the Emergency Relief Bureau of New York City during the Great Depression, and later the Associate Director of the Welfare Council of New York.

Mayo was appointed dean of the School in 1941, possessed of a passion for its important work and a real gift for communicating the many ways the wider community benefited from that work. One of his major contributions to the School was his transformation of that passion into badly needed financial support. Mayo's efforts built the School's reputation, both locally and nationally, a fact noticed by Western Reserve University, which appointed him vice president in 1949.

He left the University to become Executive Director of the Association for the Aid of Crippled Children in New York City. Influential in the fields of child welfare and, more specifically, children with disabilities, Mayo served on four White House conferences for children and youth from 1930 to 1960 and was an advisor to the Truman, Eisenhower, Kennedy, Johnson, and Ford administrations.

Mayo returned to Cleveland and his work at the School in the late 1970s. Beginning as an assistant professor, Mayo went on to become a development officer and a member of the School's Visiting Committee. In 1978, an endowed professorship in his honor, the Leonard W. Mayo Professor of Family and Child Welfare, was established, which is now held by Mark I. Singer, PhD 1983, MSSA 1979. Case Western Reserve University awarded Mayo an honorary doctorate in 1992.

to take on additional responsibility in their clinical work as they mastered theory and technique.

An example of this new model occurred in 1944, when faculty approached Bell Greve, the director of the Cuyahoga County Relief Department, and came to an agreement that students doing field placements in public welfare at the agency should begin their first year with responsibility for 15 families. The previous requirement was that new students took on fifty families, which they found to be overwhelming, and the agency found to be frustrating as it tried to balance the students' lack of experience with the immediate needs of the families. The new arrangement provided "a far more effective learning experience," since it gave students the ability to gain practical experience without drowning in unreasonable expectations. The new field work structure also accounted for closer supervision by field instructors in the first year, with more independence toward the end of the program.

The Basic Eight

By 1946, improvements in the School's curriculum kept it at the forefront of schools of social work. After much deliberation, the faculty decided to adopt a core curriculum that included what the National Association of Schools of Social Work (NASSW) would later refer to as "the basic eight"

+ SASS class, ca. 1949.

subject areas: case work, group work, community organization, public welfare, social administration, social research, medical information, and psychiatric information. NASSW recommended that these eight areas be included at the center of graduate social work education across the country. The School continued to offer additional coursework in its specializations, but required that whether students were studying child welfare or medical social work, they shared the same base of knowledge. They also considered offering courses that addressed some new areas of social work that were becoming more prominent because of World War II, including social work for veterans returning home in need of vocational, mental, and physical rehabilitation – a specialization that would receive a full-time faculty member and federal government support in the next decade.

The faculty's efforts on the role of research was also at the forefront of the field. In 1948, the

School hosted a workshop with the American Association of Social Workers to address the question of research in the social work curriculum, and how to define general social science research versus social work research. The working definition presented in the conference report stated that social science research could contribute to advancing any of the fields of social scientific inquiry. Social work research, however, "deals with the problems faced by professional social workers, and by the community in its concern with social work functions." The conference also inspired the formation of the Social Work Research Group, founded in 1949 as the first national organization to promote social work research as central to the advancement of scholarship and classroom teaching. It later became one of the founding organizations of the National Association of Social Workers.

World War II: The Greatest Responsibility

When America joined World War II in 1941, the School was immediately impacted. Dean Mayo's administrative skills were requisitioned for the role of Assistant Director of the Cuyahoga County Civilian Defense Department, and in 1943, he became the part-time Director of Civilian Mobilization in Cuyahoga County. Tasked with protecting the citizens of Northeast Ohio in the event of an air raid by enemy troops, the Council of Civilian

+ Students support the war effort. Note the "Remember Pearl Harbor" banner in the background.

Defense was responsible for organizing and training teams of emergency responders and air raid wardens, as well as for day-to-day wartime efforts, including coordinating rationing programs, scrap metal drives, rag and waste paper collection, and war savings bond promotions.

"The physical scientists have made it clear that while they can reveal and to some extent harness the terrifying forces of the Universe, they cannot discipline man in whose hands these unleashed forces now rest. The development and control of the inner man, they tell us, is the task of the social scientist.

The query as to whether mankind is equal to this supreme test is no longer an academic question. It is a sober and urgent one. It is, moreover, a question to which the best of our social scientists and social workers have long since called our attention.

Modern social work as a healing agent, a method of preventing individual, family, and community disintegration, as a rehabilitative factor in a Universe where destruction has been paramount, as an art devoted to the development of human relations, has reached its greatest hour."

—Dean Leonard W. Mayo
Annual Report, 1945–46

Many other faculty members were similarly called to national service and accepted positions in national defense programs. Their resignations put the School's reorganization efforts on the back burner and placed increased pressure on the remaining faculty. In the academic year 1941-1942, 25% of first-year students were eligible for the draft, at the same time that demand for social workers on the home front was increasing exponentially. Assistant Dean Johnson stated that "it is safe to say that the School could have placed three times the number of its graduating class" in full time social work positions.

In his first annual report in 1942, Dean Mayo wrote "It is necessary to speak briefly at the outset of the effects of the war and its demands on the school. The period through which we are now passing and the months ahead offer to social work and hence to schools of social work the greatest opportunity and responsibility in their history. Graduates of Western Reserve's School of Applied Social Sciences and of similar schools are serving in this war to a far greater extent than was true in World War I. The Red Cross, the USO, the Office of Defense, Health, and Welfare, the Office of Civilian Defense and the regular public and private social services in this and other communities throughout the country are pressing

+ Members of the U.S. V-12 Navy College Training Program march at the Case School of Applied Science, 1943.

us daily for personnel we are unable to supply."

Dean Mayo emphasized to President Leutner that the work of the School, its faculty, and its alumni was expected to increase with the ongoing war and its eventual end. Trained social workers would be desperately needed at the conclusion of the war for the purposes of rehabilitation and community organization both at home and abroad. He also pointed out that the collaborative and advisory role many faculty provided for community agencies was being called on in the service of national defense and the war effort at home.

Although additional responsibilities reduced the amount of time faculty had available, Dean Mayo stated that "the manner and spirit in which they have carried the increasingly heavy duties of the School in addition are a tribute to their devotion and capacity as citizens and social workers."

Accelerated Program: 1941–1947

An example of the faculty and administration's response to the intense demands of wartime and the need for trained graduates across disciplines was their vote to adopt an accelerated plan of study that would allow students to complete coursework in 16 rather than 24 months. It required the School to operate year-round on a trimester system, with students accepted on a rolling basis to one of the three terms beginning in June, October, or February.

In practice, this was positive for students and the organizations that needed them—such as the Red Cross, the USO, and the Office of Defense, Health and Welfare—but it seriously taxed the resources of the School. In the 1946 Annual Report, Dean Mayo estimated that the faculty were working an average of 51 hours per week, just to keep up with teaching, advising, and community responsibilities.

In Greater Demand than Ever

By 1943, SASS students and alumni were in greater demand than ever before. Expansion of public welfare services, openings created because of the draft in public and private social welfare agencies, and the needs of government agencies in wartime drove the need for accelerated training and placement. At the same time, opportunities in industry and the military that had not been open to women were creating competition for potential students. The School embarked on an ambitious recruitment effort in partnership with the Frances Payne Bolton School of Nursing. Armed with a new full color 15-minute movie that illustrated typical activities of social workers, Assistant Dean Johnson traveled to undergraduate institutions around the state and across the country seeking new students.

Dean Mayo was also collaborating with university colleagues on a committee to organize a series

ALUMNI PROFILES:
The Fabulous 1940s

+ **Irene Sogg, MSSA 1940:** Her legacy endures in the Irene Sogg Gross Service Award, which is awarded each commencement to a member of the graduating class by their peers for outstanding interest and accomplishments in humanitarian service.

+ **Jean Maxwell, MSSA 1941 | NASW Social Work Pioneer:** She played a central role in establishing the field of gerontology within social work and spent a significant portion of her career at the National Federation of Settlements and Neighborhood Centers.

+ **Hope Griswold Curfman, MSSA 1942:** In 1962, she helped to found the Hope Center in Denver, providing services to special needs students and autistic children. After the tragic loss of her daughter, she and her husband established the Grief Education Institute.

+ **Eleanor Weisberger Weintraub, MSSA 1943:** An emeritus faculty member of Case Western Reserve School of Medicine, she pioneered the use of parental support groups and co-taught with Dr. Benjamin Spock, who wrote the introduction to her book, *Your Young Child and You.*

+ **Margaret E. Adams, MSSA 1944 | NASW Social Work Pioneer:** After deciding to attend SASS after meeting Grace Coyle at a conference, Adams became a founding staff member of NASW and helped to establish the Council on Social Work Education.

+ **Margaret A. Golton, BA 1931, MSSA 1945, DSW 1964:** A three-time alumna of Western Reserve University, Golton was the author of numerous publications, including *Your Brain at Work: A New View of Personality and Behavior.*

+ **Jean Greenhaigh, MSSA 1946:** A psychiatric social worker, Greenhaigh helped coordinate community-based mental health care in California, where the state legislature honored her as Woman of the Year in 1987.

+ **Dorothy Burnside, MSSA 1947:** Director of West Virginia's child welfare program and later Assistant Commissioner of the Department of Human Services, she professionalized the state's children's services and was a major force in adoption policy development.

+ **Margarita Electra Rivas Huantes, MSSA 1948:** Driven to enter social work after seeing the needs of migrant agricultural laborers, Huantes focused her career on adult literacy and services for the Mexican immigrant community in Texas.

+ **Lillian Milanof, MSSA 1949 | NASW Social Work Pioneer:** A nationally recognized expert in child welfare and professor emerita of the Raymond A. Kent School of Social Work at the University of Louisville, she was awarded an honorary doctorate by Spalding University.

+ Dorothy E. Allen Burnside, MSSA 1947, in March 1945.

of courses designed to prepare students for work in the postwar rehabilitation of Europe and other countries, in cooperation with the Office of Foreign Relief and Rehabilitation. The School created a special course in introductory case work for local Red Cross workers at the request of the agency.

Demands on faculty continued to increase, even as full-time members of the staff decreased from 17 in 1941 to 13 in 1943. Florence Day, one of the founding faculty in case work, left the school to become dean of the Smith School for Social Work, and three others were called to other duties due to shortages in social welfare agency staff and administration.

Alumni and the War Effort

While dedication to the war effort redirected faculty attention, Dean Mayo and Assistant Dean Johnson made an effort to reach out to school alumni for help in funding scholarships, endowment, and a new building. In June 1941, more than 125 alumni gathered at the annual meeting of the National Conference of Social Work to hear about the activities of the school and meet its new dean over breakfast in Atlantic City.

As World War II continued, alumni wrote in to share the activities in which they were engaged. From all over the United States and the world came reports of alumni directing USO units, Red

Cross Field and Rest Camps, providing recreational opportunities for military personnel, supportive services to army chaplains, and assisting medical doctors and psychiatrists working to rehabilitate soldiers after combat. Even demands on family casework and child welfare workers increased during the war, reflecting the growing need for quality day care for young children, assistance for families impacted by the war, and help for returning veterans readjusting to home life. For the latter, medical and psychiatric social workers were also in demand by soldiers suffering from mental and physical disabilities after their service.

Agencies also expected social workers to have recreational program skills to facilitate group work in settings such as the USO, YWCA, or summer camps. Thanks to a generous donor, group worker students had a new space on campus in the basement of Euclid Hall to practice recreational activities. There students learned "program skills," including arts, crafts, and how to lead songs and games. Some students, however, rebelled against the idea that their graduate education should include learning the words to children's songs or how to make art projects out of papier-mâché.

After the end of World War II, enrollment at the School swelled as returning veterans utilized the G.I. Bill to pay for graduate education. In 1947, the incoming class of 107 full-time students was the largest to date. Of the 107 students, 27 were men and 22 were veterans. Including extension courses and part-time students, the School had a total enrollment of almost 700 individuals.

In 1948, Dean Mayo accepted a position as Vice President of Western Reserve University. His successor, Donald V. Wilson, had extensive experience in settlement houses and welfare work before being drafted into the U.S. Army, where he ultimately became responsible for creating welfare services for the country of Japan under the military government of the United States Army. The faculty were enthusiastic about Dean Wilson's appointment, but he was at the School less than a year.

Assistant Dean Johnson was selected to succeed Dean Wilson. As an alumna, longtime faculty member, and mainstay of the School, Johnson was the first female dean of the School of Applied Social Sciences, and she would lead the School into a new era and a new home on campus. +

Dean, 1948–1949
DONALD V. WILSON, JD, PhD
The Democracy of Social Work

Dean for just one year, Donald V. Wilson came to the School after a distinguished academic and military career.

Wilson served as director of the social work training branch of the Public Health and Welfare Section to the Supreme Commander of Allied Powers, General Douglas MacArthur, in postwar Japan. In just two years, Wilson helped to establish Japan's systems of "old age" insurance, public assistance, child welfare services and juvenile courts, and health centers. He also helped create two schools of social work, one of which became the Japan College of Social Work in Tokyo.

Wilson viewed the new roles of social workers in the postwar period as crucial to the stability of governments in former combat zones across the world. He wrote "the term 'democracy,' which is used so freely, has real meaning for parents when better food, clothing and health are provided for their children, but means little to those without these essentials. Social welfare programs can help make the word 'democracy' to be more than an abstract political theory."

+ Dean Donald V. Wilson.

1950

Cleveland Browns
join National
Football League and
win league title

1952

Dwight D. Eisenhower
elected President

1954

Brown v. Board of
Education Supreme
Court case

1956

Federal Highway
Act passed

1958

St. Lawrence
Seaway completed

Julius and Ethel
Rosenberg convicted
of espionage

1951

Montgomery bus
boycott begins

1955

Fidel Castro seizes
power in Cuba

1959

Korean War ends

1953

Civil Rights Act of
1957 passed

1957

CHRONOLOGY 1950–1959

CHAPTER 4

A Home of Our Own

The School of Applied Social Sciences entered the 1950s with the appointment of its first social administration master's graduate, Margaret H. Johnson, MSSA 1919, as its first female dean, who was guiding the School into its first permanent home, Beaumont Hall, in 1951.

Upon succeeding Wilson, Dean Johnson's primary task was to address the School's continuing budget deficits. University President John S. Millis, as part of an ongoing project to streamline and unify the professional schools and departments, examined SASS and concluded its organizational structure was too diffuse, causing faculty to be too divided between students, committee obligations, and community service. In 1952, Millis requested that SASS "conduct a searching study of the program and operations of the School."

Soul-Searching Self-Study

Dean Johnson and the faculty viewed Millis' request for a self-study as an opportunity to update the educational programs to incorporate the latest trends in professional social work. SASS had already begun to expand its offerings with the creation of the Advanced Program in 1952. The self-study, begun that same year, was conducted entirely in-house by faculty and staff. Historian Thomas F. Campbell characterized it as "the most soul-searching examination of its program that the School had ever undertaken."

The self-study also reflected a larger current in social work, as practitioners nationally were similarly engaged with the question of how social work should address contemporary developments. A 1951 report for the National Council on Social Work Education examined the relationship between social work and urbanization, changes in social work practices and agencies, the international role of the United States, and develop-

+ Dean Margaret H. Johnson in front of 2117 Adelbert Road, one of the School's "Five Little Houses."

Dean, 1950–1958
MARGARET H. JOHNSON, AB 1917, MSSA 1919
A Legacy of Firsts

That the first person to receive the Master of Science with the designation in Social Administration degree in 1919 became the School's first female Dean reflects what a vital role Margaret H. Johnson had in the growth and development of the School from 1917 to 1958—as a student, faculty member, alumna, and visionary leader.

Upon graduation, Johnson began her social work career assisting immigrant workers, then became executive secretary of the Cleveland chapter of the League of Women Voters. She moved to Washington, D.C., in 1924 to take the position of assistant executive secretary of the National League of Women Voters.

Johnson returned to the School in 1927, when she was hired as Executive Secretary for Dean Cutler. Three years later, she was appointed Assistant Dean, then served as an Instructor, Assistant Professor, and Associate Professor. In 1939, Johnson was promoted to Professor, shortly after she helped create the School's Alumni Association.

Johnson's familiarity with administration and faculty, her tireless commitment to students and alumni, and her vision for the School led Johnson to be appointed Dean in 1950. Under her leadership, Beaumont Hall—the School's first dedicated building on campus—was funded and built in 1951, and the doctoral program was founded in 1952. Dean Johnson served on many influential local and national boards and was chairperson of the American Association of Social Workers.

Upon her retirement in 1958, Johnson said, "The School of Applied [Social] Sciences has developed greatly in the last few years. This development, especially the revised program and the new building, gives me a feeling of great satisfaction."

Described by Western Reserve University President John S. Millis as "the Sassy Dean from SASS," Johnson was also honored at the 75th Convocation of the Flora Stone Mather College for Women in 1963. She was awarded an honorary degree from Western Reserve University in 1966. Johnson died in 1976 at the age of 82.

+ Margaret H. Johnson.

ments in the social sciences. Faculty used this report as guidance for their self-study, forming committees that consulted with national social work leadership, social work practitioners, alumni, and students regarding the future direction of the School.

In a paper delivered to the Council on Social Work Education in 1952, Grace Longwell Coyle described the considerations behind the self-study: balancing the practice courses and field work with other coursework, instilling social workers with the traditions of the profession, providing needed social services to the community, incorporating the latest developments in the social sciences, and including research as a key part of social work practice.

New Curriculum Attracts National Attention

In 1953, the School published the results of the self-study, recommending the creation of a curriculum designed to provide students with "a basic core of knowledge concerning society, social work methods and the purposes of social work in society." Launched in the fall of 1954, it consisted of core courses that all students were required to take before they majored in either social casework or social group work, with a community organization concentration added in the late 1950s. The new courses were:

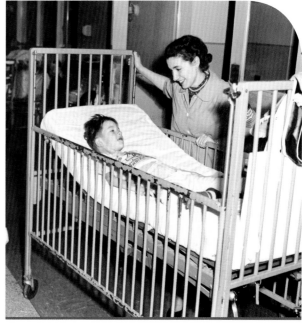

+ **Left:** The faculty of the School of Applied Social Sciences, 1954. **Right:** Faculty member Constance Impallari Albee at the side of a child client, 1950.

- Dynamics of Social Process I and II
- Social Welfare Organizations I, II, and III
- Individual Growth and Development I and II
- Introduction to Social Work Practice
- Social Casework I
- Social Group Work I
- Research in Social Work I, II, and III
- Seminar: The Social Work Profession
- Field Practice

In 1959-60, Research in Social Work I, II, and III were revised to Introduction to Research Methodology, Measurement and Statistics in Social Work Research, and Practicum in Social Work Research. By the end of the decade, the School expanded the core curriculum to add courses in psychopathology and physical illness, community organization, administration, and legal issues.

In their second year of study, social casework and social group work students took four additional classes in their field, and community organization students took one additional course. The field work program was also redesigned and limited a first-year student's placement to two days per week instead of three during the first semester. The School also worked with field agencies to develop a comprehensive student orientation program and created additional continuing education courses for field instructors.

The School's new curriculum was well-received nationally. After faculty presented a report on the changes to the annual meeting of the Council of Social Work Education, Dean Johnson received multiple inquiries from American and Canadian schools requesting more information. Four schools even sent visitors for observation of classes. The Russell Sage Foundation also awarded the School a three-year grant to research how recent findings in the social sciences could be ap-

DOCTORAL PROGRAM FOUNDED IN 1952

The doctoral program was established in 1952, making SASS among the first five schools of social work in the United States to offer a doctorate. It was created for students "capable of giving a high level of leadership, especially through teaching and research."

Coursework included training in the history of social work, current issues, psychiatry, research, community organization, staff development, social casework, group work, and principles and methods in social work education. A unique feature of the program was the requirement to take social sciences courses from other areas of the university. Upon completion, students were awarded a Doctor of Social Work (DSW).

Initially, the doctorate was offered as a component of the School's "Advanced Program," which gave master's students the option to pursue a doctoral degree or a special third year program that provided an additional year of field work and courses—an appealing opportunity for experienced social workers who had already earned their master's degree. Upon completion, students in the third year program received a Dean's Certificate and could apply their coursework toward a doctorate, if they later chose to pursue the DSW. The first Dean's Certificates for the third year program were awarded in 1953 to Martha Ramsay Erbaugh and Verl S. Lewis, MSSA 1939. In 1954, Lewis would earn the School's first DSW.

Faculty continued to refine and innovate coursework in the doctoral program. The curriculum was revised in 1965 to emphasize research and training in one of three career tracks: researcher, teacher of social work methods, or expert in administration and social policy. That same year, the degree conferred was changed to a Doctor of Philosophy in Social Welfare (PhD). Further innovation came in the 1980s with the introduction of the Intensive Semester, a first-of-its-kind program which allowed students to pursue doctoral work during the summer and part-time (see Chapter 7).

Today, the doctoral program remains the cornerstone of the Mandel School, providing students with a supportive educational environment, increased opportunities for participation in funded research, and an innovative curriculum that prepares social work leaders who demonstrate competency in research, social welfare theory, teaching, and leadership.

port also recommended the hiring of an Assistant Dean and a full-time admissions officer.

Improvements in Enrollment and Finances

During the 1950s, there was a decrease in enrollment at schools of social work across the nation. This also proved true for SASS at the beginning of the decade, although it remained one of the seven largest schools of social work in America.

While the majority of students continued to come from Greater Cleveland or Ohio, more than 20 states and six countries were represented by the student body throughout the 1950s, with male enrollment hovering around 30%. The majority of students were enrolled in the social case work program. By the end of the decade, enrollment improved considerably, due in large part to a series of student recruitment campaigns. Enrollment in the master's program and part-time students increasing by 50% between 1958 and 1959, and the doctoral program expanded from five students to 20. In conjunction with the Welfare Foundation and the Cleveland Foundation, the School created a "Career Opportunity" office to encourage people to pursue careers in social work and hosted a Career Day for undergraduates at Western Reserve University.

By the mid-1950s, the School's finances also began to improve, as it received grants-in-aid from

plied to social work curricula, a study that was led by sociologist Joseph Eaton.

To address the criticism that the faculty were overextended, the School now required that faculty work a forty-hour week, engage in more research, and not undertake outside community service without Dean Johnson's approval. The administr-

ative structure was also restructured to include the dean and a series of faculty committees: Committee of the Whole, General Faculty Committee (consisting of full-time faculty who were Assistant Professors or higher), and four standing committees (Administrative Policies, Classroom Program, Field Program, and Advising). The self-study re-

+ Students attending class in Beaumont Hall, 1950s.

BEAUMONT HALL

It became increasingly clear throughout the 1940s that, with an enrollment of more than 200 students, the School had outgrown the "five little houses" on Adelbert Road, which it had called home since the late 1920s. It was in dire need of additional classroom, office, and library space—in 1946, the librarian feared that moving additional bookshelves into their already crowded area would cause the floor to collapse.

Dean Mayo lamented the "urgent if not desperate need for a new building," and created an Advanced Committee on the Future of the School, which was tasked with finding donors to finance construction. A new building for SASS became a key component of Western Reserve University's 125th anniversary fundraising campaign begun in 1950.

Located at 2035 Abington Road (now University Hospitals Drive), Beaumont Hall was built in 1951 and named for the Louis D. Beaumont Foundation, which provided significant funding for construction. Beaumont was co-founder of The May Company, a popular chain of department stores headquartered in Cleveland. The new building included classrooms, faculty and administrative offices, a dedicated space for the library, and a legendary student lounge still fondly recalled by alumni. The Student Association provided a series of gifts throughout the decade to make the building feel more like home, including furniture, a radio and record player, and a much-needed loudspeaker system.

Beaumont Hall was the School's home until 1990, when it relocated to its current building on the corner of Ford Drive and Bellflower Road. The Beaumont Hall building was demolished, and its site is now part of University Hospitals of Cleveland.

+ **Top left:** Dean Johnson watches the construction of Beaumont Hall, 1950. **Top right:** Former Dean James E. Cutler addresses the crowd at the cornerstone laying for Beaumont Hall on April 26, 1951. **Bottom left:** Former Dean James E. Cutler, Western Reserve University President John S. Millis, former Dean Leonard W. Mayo, and Dean Margaret H. Johnson at the cornerstone laying ceremony for Beaumont Hall. **Bottom right:** Beaumont Hall.

+ Class of 1954 outside Beaumont Hall.

+ Alumni leading fundraising efforts.

several social agencies, a three-year award from the Welfare Federation for student financial aid, and generous donations from friends and alumni for scholarships. With President Millis' blessing, the School also began a $2 million endowment drive. The Alumni Association was active in fundraising for the endowment, raising $35,000 in the first year.

"In the space of one short year SASS has moved significantly away from being a poor member of the family of schools within Western Reserve University to a status of greater self-support, independence and recognition," noted Alumni Association President Richard E. Stover, MSSA 1949.

Visiting Committee Founded and More Alumni Engaged

As another component of the self-study, President Millis and the Board of Trustees created a Visiting Committee for the School to replace its existing Advisory Committee. The new committee included more community members and provided a direct connection between the School and the Board of Western Reserve University. Tasked with advising the School regarding curriculum, research, and building strong community relationships, the first Visiting Committee chairperson was civic activist and university trustee Dorothy Prentiss Schmitt. Schmitt would later endow a professorship and was also a member of the University's Board of

Trustees. In 1958, she was joined on the board by Frank J. Hertel, MSSA 1934, General Director of the Community Service Society of New York.

Realizing that the majority of alumni lived outside the Cleveland area, the Alumni Association redesigned its bylaws in 1959 to include a National Advisory Board that held regional meetings and assisted in fundraising and student recruitment. The association also established a memorial fund for contributions made in honor of deceased alumni. The School created an additional memorial fund named for Thelma Wertheim, to aid the library.

The new Visiting Committee—which quickly became an integral part of the School's administration and a strong voice in both guiding policy and programs—proved to be a significant help in fundraising as well. W.C. Treuhaft, a prominent Cleveland businessman, succeeded Schmitt as chair and under his leadership the committee raised more than $250,000 for the endowment by 1958. At the decade's end, the School's fundraising efforts were so successful that they embarked upon a new campaign to create the first endowed chair, named in honor of Grace Longwell Coyle.

Growth in Research Funding and International Activity

Throughout the 1950s, faculty were active in research and outreach projects that were attracting

DON'T FORGET: Advice to Incoming Students from the 1957 Student Handbook

A typewriter – to type the volume of pages,
And clothing – to meet those rapid weather changes.
For study – bulbs and a good desk lamp,
A raincoat and hat to keep out the damp;
For keeping in touch with home, plenty of stationary;
For the words you can't spell – a dictionary.
A loud alarm for rousing you, and sturdy boots
for Cleveland dew.
A record player and radio,
And don't forget to bring some dough!

In 1956, furnished room rent averaged $35 per month and ranged from $26 to $45. Furnished apartment rent averaged $95 and ranged from $70 to $160 (including utilities) with two to four students sharing the rental.

The newly opened Student Union provides a snack bar for light lunches. Wade's Drug, Marshall's Drug, or Dorsel's (conveniently located within a block or so of school) also serve light lunches, reasonably priced. If you care to venture further away (perhaps on your way to a bank) there is The Brick Cottage, Howard Johnson's, the Tasty Shop, and Clarks. Back to reality and those day-to-day lunches, bring your own and enjoy it with the rest of the gang in the Student Lounge amid card games, ping pong, gab fests, and last minute assignments!

There's usually something going on at SASS among the students. The Social Committee sponsors a picnic during orientation week and another one in May, plus several social functions during the year. Pete Seeger usually makes an annual appearance at the students' request.

ALUMNI PROFILE:
Eliezer Jaffe, MSSA 1957, DSW 1960

Eliezer Jaffe is emblematic of the outsized impact alumni have had on social work education nationally and internationally. He was the first person to introduce the study of the nonprofit sector, fundraising, and philanthropy into university curriculum, and he published *Giving Wisely*, the first Directory of Nonprofit Organizations in Israel, which influenced government policy and led to broad transparency in the sector.

Called the "father of Israeli social work," Jaffe was the author of 14 books spanning child welfare, community development, and nonprofit organizations and philanthropy. He was the Director of the Jerusalem Social Service Department, where he instituted social policy changes and services which spread across the country, and was one of the founders of the Paul Baerwald School of Social Work and Social Welfare. In 1990, Jaffe founded the Israel Free Loan Association, which has provided more than $170 million in interest-free loans to the working poor and struggling small businesses.

Upon his death in 2017, he was the Centraide L. Jacques Menard Professor Emeritus for the Study of Volunteering, Nonprofit Organizations, and Philanthropy at the Hebrew University of Jerusalem.

+ Eliezer Jaffe, MSSA 1957, DSW 1960.

both foundation and federal funding. The Cleveland Foundation assisted the School with the creation and promotion of the Institute on the Prevention and Treatment of Juvenile Delinquency in 1954-55. That same year, Hope Williams, MSSA 1947, was hired as an assistant professor with funding from the Federal Office of Vocational Rehabilitation, which also provided financial assistance to student trainees who studied rehabilitation case work. Norman Polansky, MSSA 1943, and clinical psychologist Erwin Weiss received a grant from the National Institutes of Health to study how the climate of institutions affected children's access to treatment, conducted in collaboration with Bellefaire Jewish Children's Bureau.

In 1956-57, the School received a $90,000 grant from the U.S. Public Health Service and proposed creating a center "to be concerned with the basic research in the practices and processes of social work." SASS also partnered with the Western Reserve University School of Medicine and Department of Education to begin a program for nursery school preparation, and collaborated with other University departments on projects such as the Intergroup Relations Workshop.

One such collaboration was the Institute on the Care of the Aged and Chronically Ill in Philanthropic, Private and County Homes. Funded by the Ford Foundation and the Welfare Federation, the institute was led by Irving Rosow, who held a dual appointment at SASS and Western Reserve University's sociology department.

International activity also expanded during the 1950s, with the School hosting visitors from Malaysia and Jordan. Faculty member Clyde White taught in Thailand on a Fulbright scholarship; on his trip home to the United States, he visited a community development project in Egypt. Coyle spent the 1957-58 school year on sabbatical, teaching and attending conferences in England, Switzerland, Denmark, Sweden, the Netherlands, Italy, and Greece. Locally, the School began a cooperative program in 1956 with the Cleveland International Program for Youth Leaders and Social Workers (CIP) to encourage international students to attend the School. Students in the program spent six months studying at SASS, then worked at local summer camps.

Faculty Rise to Prominence

Faculty played prominent roles in the social work profession in Ohio and nationally. Coyle was elected president of the Council of Social Work Education of the United States and Canada. Ray Fisher, MSSA 1939, served as the head of the National Association of Social Workers in Cleveland. Esther Test, MSSA 1938; Virginia Tamar; and Kaye Weitzel, MSSA 1941, participated in Council on Social

+ Faculty in 1958.

+ Dean Johnson's retirement dinner in 1958. **Top:** Dean Johnson, Myra Thomas, and Angela Trannett. **Bottom:** Dinner guests.

Work Education and National Association of Social Workers committees.

A series of new faculty hires happened throughout the decade, including alumni Mary Louise Somers, BA 1937, MSSA 1943, DSW 1957; Roger Rowles Miller, MSSA 1949, DSW 1957; and future dean John Turner, MSSA 1948, DSW 1959, who was instrumental in creating the community organization major. Dr. Benjamin M. Spock, later nationally known for his books on child care, joined the Western Reserve University faculty in 1955 and taught growth and development courses for SASS students, in addition to his responsibilities at the School of Medicine.

A series of retirements also occurred during the late 1950s. Many faculty members retired who were instrumental in the establishment of the School, including Agnes Schroeder, Anna Belle Tracy, and Helen Walker.

But the most significant retirement happened in 1958. Dean Margaret Johnson retired and was succeeded by Nathan E. Cohen, Associate Dean of Columbia University's New York School of Social Work. In May 1958, Dean Johnson was honored at

+ Nathan E. Cohen in October 1962.

Dean, 1958–1963 | NASW Social Work Pioneer
NATHAN E. COHEN, PhD
Devoted to the Expansion of
Social Work Education

Appointed the School's fifth Dean in 1958, Nathan E. Cohen came from the New York School of Social Work at Columbia University, where he had been a faculty member for ten years. He earned his bachelor's, master's, and doctoral degrees in psychology from Harvard University.

Honored as a Social Work Pioneer by the National Association of Social Workers, Cohen served as the organization's first president from 1955 to 1957. He was president of the American Association of Schools of Social Work (the predecessor of the Council on Social Work Education) and the National Conference on Social Welfare. Cohen also was a consultant to the National Institutes of Mental Health and the Children's Bureau.

While Dean, Cohen expanded the School's relations with community organizations and within the University, helping to establish financial aid opportunities for students and investing in the creation of research-based centers. He was appointed Vice President of Western Reserve University in 1962. Later he became Dean of the School of Welfare at the University of California at Los Angeles, from which he retired in the 1980s. Cohen is the author of two books, *Social Work in the American Tradition* and *Citizen Volunteer.*

a retirement banquet attended by 175 guests. The Alumni Association presented her with a $1,500 check and a scrapbook with messages of thanks and well-wishes from alumni. The School dedicated a new library table and chairs in her honor, complete with a commemorative plaque. In Dean Johnson's thank you note to the alumni, she commented with her trademark wit that "the Library chairs and table, with its memorial plaque, should convince future generations of students that there once was a woman dean."

By 1960, the School of Applied Social Sciences continued to be at the forefront of social work education nationally and internationally, yet continued its significant local and community engagement. With new curriculum and research projects in place, the School was prepared to address the expanding field of social work—and the turbulent decade ahead. +

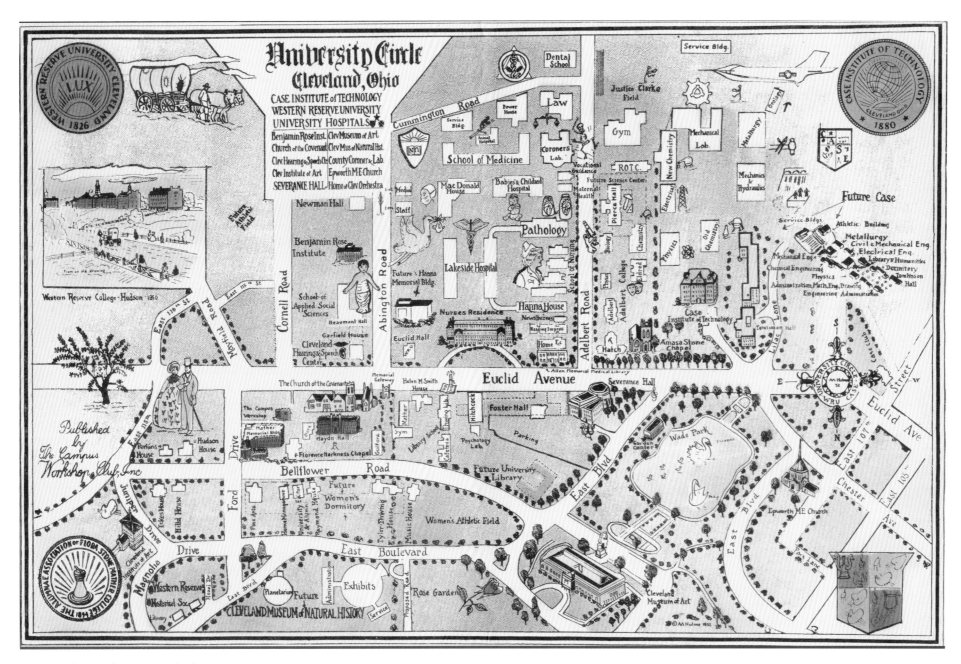

+ Pictorial Map of University Circle, 1950s.

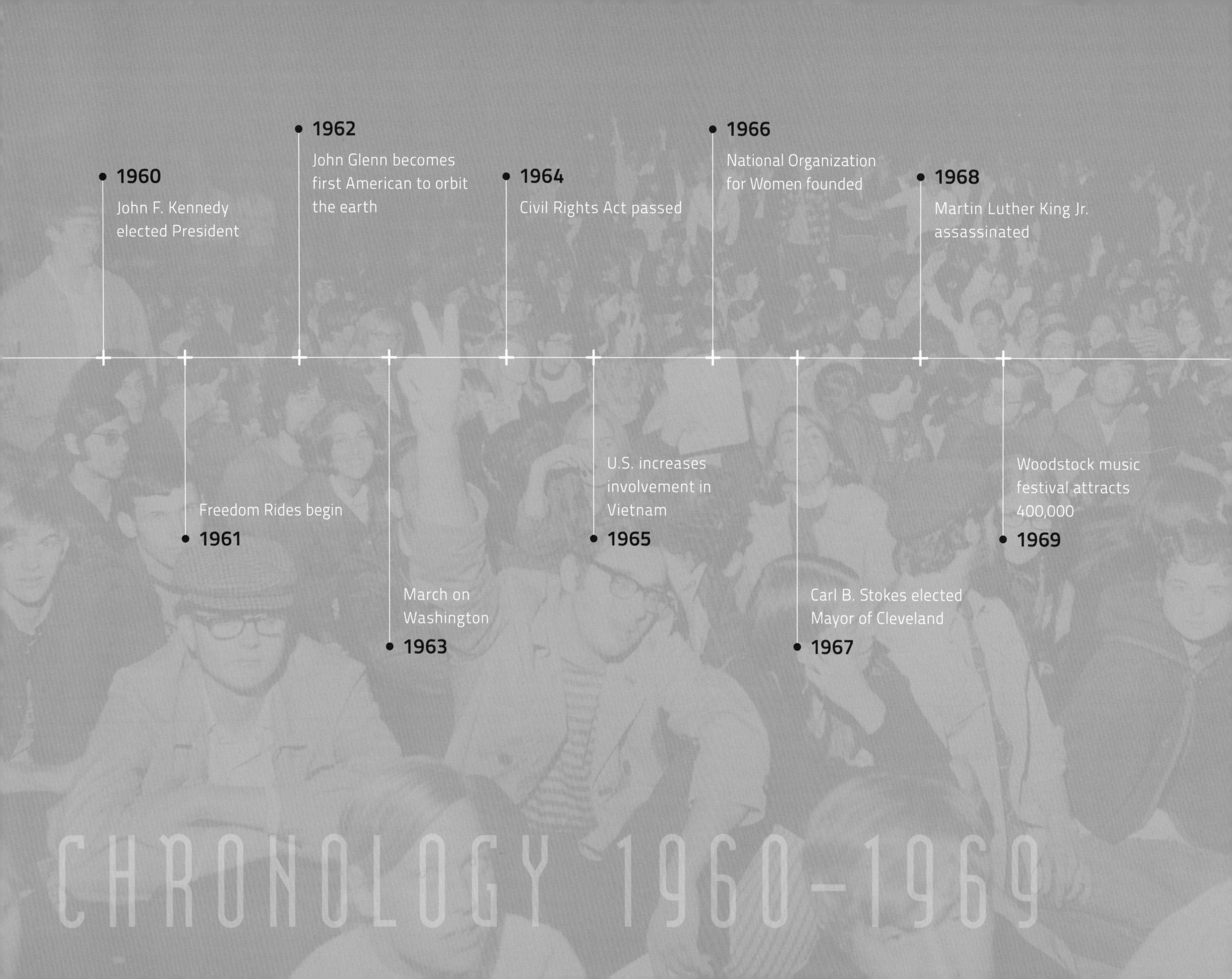

1960
John F. Kennedy
elected President

1962
John Glenn becomes
first American to orbit
the earth

1964
Civil Rights Act passed

1966
National Organization
for Women founded

1968
Martin Luther King Jr.
assassinated

Freedom Rides begin
1961

U.S. increases
involvement in
Vietnam
1965

Woodstock music
festival attracts
400,000
1969

March on
Washington
1963

Carl B. Stokes elected
Mayor of Cleveland
1967

CHRONOLOGY 1960–1969

CHAPTER 5

Making Voices Heard

As the decade dawned in 1960, Western Reserve University and the Case Institute of Technology were enmeshed in national and international events. Nationally, the election of President John F. Kennedy and the advancement of the space program set the stage for what looked to be a decade of limitless possibilities. Both universities continued to grow and innovate, and their administrations began to discuss the possibility of creating a federation between the schools. It culminated in their merger in 1967 and the creation of Case Western Reserve University.

Optimism in a New Decade

At the School of Applied Social Sciences, Dean Cohen reported in the fall of 1960 that enrollment in the master's program was up 30%, the quality of applicants was increasing, and enrollment in the advanced/doctoral program had doubled from the previous year. He also noted that the vast majority of the School's field placement agencies had agreed to pool their student grants into a central fellowship fund that the School could distribute based on student need. Working on subsidy arrangements with field placement organizations had been an ongoing negotiation between organizations that wanted to have more control over the students assigned to them, and the School, which wanted greater flexibility over student funding and field placements.

New endeavors included the creation of a Research Institute with a generous grant from the Cleveland Foundation, which helped coordinate faculty research projects, provide students with training in research methods and interpretation, and centralize grant administration. Projects already underway included a study of access to mental health treatment by Norman Polansky, MSSA 1943, conducted at Bellefaire Jewish Children's Bureau and funded by the National Insti-

tute of Mental Health, as well as a study of the elderly in public housing led by Irving Rosow, which was a joint venture with the Welfare Federation and funded by the Ford Foundation. The School also developed programs with the Garden Valley Neighborhood Center and Mt. Pleasant Community Center designed to provide students with field work opportunities while meeting community needs. These kinds of collaborative demonstration projects continued a tradition of community-based research that began in the School's early years. The results from these projects were used to inform national policymakers about effective social policies for addressing disadvantaged populations.

Under the leadership of faculty member John B. Turner, MSSA 1948, DSW 1959, the community organization program was reinvented with a tailored series of classes paired with field placements at either the Cleveland Welfare Federation or the Jewish Federation in their respective departments dedicated to community planning—ideal settings for students to learn about the complexity of assessing community needs, addressing those needs with specific programs, and measuring program outcomes. Strengthening the relationship between the School and these agencies was the fact that alumni led them: Henry L. Zucker, MSSA 1935, was Executive Director of the Jewish Federation and William T. McCullough, MSSA 1966, directed the Welfare Federation. Additionally, in 1965, the school received a significant grant from the Cleveland Foundation to create a training program in community organization in conjunction with the Urban League.

A Great Society

With the assassination of President John F. Kennedy on November 22, 1963, the optimism of the early part of the decade was eclipsed by tragedy. In its aftermath, President Lyndon B. Johnson launched his vision for a Great Society, based in part on Kennedy's New Frontier, which foresaw an America in which access to opportunity was not limited by race, poverty, or geography.

In late 1964, in his regular column in the SASS Newsletter, Dean Cohen exhorted students to remain committed to action in the face of terrible events. He characterized Kennedy's agenda as recognizing "the major issues of poverty, disease, unemployment, civil rights, educational and cultural deprivation," and that trying to address those issues would build a stronger foundation for a more democratic, and thereby more inclusive, society.

+ Faculty members McPherson, Hartford, Turner, Werner, and Main confer.

"These problems, created out of yesterday's blind spots and fears of change, will not find their answers in yesterday's solutions. They call for bold, courageous and adventurous ideas and actions rather than the dogmas of the past.... Those of us who are concerned with people—how they fare and how they might fare better—cannot afford the luxury of apathy and indifference."

Dean Cohen set the tone for how the School would approach the rest of the turbulent 1960s. Rather than retreating to the ivory tower, the School and its constituents would increase their engagement in Cleveland and abroad. In field placements, in the classroom, on commissions and nonprofit boards, and in the conduct and dissemination of research, SASS continued to invest in creating connections and implementing positive change.

Dean Cohen served until 1964, when he was appointed Vice President of Western Reserve University. Cohen was succeeded as dean by Herman D. Stein, whom he had known through the National Association of Social Work. Stein continued Cohen's direction for the School to examine its role in the political and civil rights concerns that characterized the decade.

The Great Society legislation passed during Lyndon Johnson's administration included the Civil

Dean, 1964–1968 | NASW Social Work Pioneer
HERMAN D. STEIN, DSW
A Lifetime of Achievement in Social Work

Herman D. Stein is renowned as an historic social work educator, administrator, consultant, and researcher. He was born on August 13, 1917, in New York City. Despite a fondness for acting and a lifelong friendship with Danny Kaye, he left the theater behind to earn his MSW in 1941 and his DSW in 1958 from the Columbia University School of Social Work (CUSSW). Thus began his career as an agency case worker and CUSSW faculty member.

In 1947, he went to Europe with his wife to work for the American Jewish Joint Distribution Committee, which was addressing the refugee crisis after World War II. He helped to establish schools of social work in Paris and Jerusalem, anticipating the need for trained social workers to help rebuild individuals and society after the trauma of the Holocaust and the war.

In 1950 he returned to New York as director of CUSSW's research center. He began his lifelong association with UNICEF in 1962 and was an advisor on community development in Tanganyika (now Tanzania), where he worked on the mental health needs of children. He designed some of the first social work courses on comparative social welfare that emphasized the Third World.

Stein came to Case Western Reserve University's School of Applied Social Sciences in 1964. Over a long career, he served as a Professor of Social Administration, Coordinator of Social and Behavioral Science, Dean, Provost of the University, University Vice President, and Distinguished University Professor. He was awarded the University Medal, Case Western Reserve University's highest honor, for his leadership and expert judgment guiding the University through the turbulence of the 1960s.

As the first dean with a doctorate in social welfare, Stein represented the new maturity and scope of a profession whose horizons had broadened to encompass a worldwide perspective on problems of social welfare. Although international students had been enrolled since the 1920s, Dean Stein's experience overseas and knowledge of social work needs in other parts of the world boosted the educational program for international students. Today, the Herman D. Stein Lecture in International Social Welfare brings an international social work scholar to the School every other year.

Stein received countless lifetime achievement awards and was inducted into several halls of fame. He passed away in 2009.

+ Dean Herman Stein.

+ Dean Herman Stein.

Rights Act, the Economic Opportunity Act, the Voting Rights Act, and the creation of Medicare and Medicaid. In the social work community, practitioners saw these initiatives as concrete steps toward addressing issues that trapped people in vulnerable communities—minorities, the poor, the elderly, and dependent children. New federal dollars came into these communities through community action grants, housing programs, expanded health coverage for the elderly and poor children, and early childhood education initiatives like Head Start.

Faculty, students, staff, and alumni were integral to implementing these programs locally and nationally. Additionally, Dean Stein was a member of Cleveland Mayor Carl B. Stokes' Advisory Committee to the Federal Office of Economic Opportunity Poverty Program and the Executive Task Force on Manpower for Comprehensive Mental Health Planning for the State of Ohio. Margaret Hartford was the Leader of the Institute on Racial Practices for the Girl Scouts.

Under the direction of Ruth Werner, the School formally established a Field Work Department to manage the increasing number of master's students and the demands of recruiting field instructors, as well as to ensure that placements were both beneficial for agencies and educational for students.

The federation of Case Western Reserve University in 1967 also made an impact on the School, leading to the promotion to Provost in 1968 of Dean Stein, who was deemed uniquely qualified to help bring together two disparate organizations. Associate Dean John B. Turner succeeded Stein as Dean, and worked to further the School's tradition of community engagement and outreach, particularly as Cleveland and the nation entered the turbulent late 1960s.

Conflagration in the City

Case Western Reserve's home, University Circle, is adjacent to two of Cleveland's urban neighborhoods, Hough and Glenville. In the 1960s, federal redlining practices, block-busting by unscrupulous realtors, increasing unemployment, and years of neglect by city administrators had left these neighborhoods with deteriorating and overcrowded housing, abysmal schools, and little hope of improvement. Strained relationships between white police and black residents due to a history of unfair and uneven law enforcement exacerbated the situation.

Sparked by a white bar owner refusing to serve black patrons on a hot summer's day in 1966, the Hough Riots resulted in widespread looting and arson. Four people died during the unrest, and order was restored only with the arrival of the National

Dean, 1968–1973 | NASW Social Work Pioneer
JOHN B. TURNER, MSSA 1948, DSW 1959
From Tuskegee Airman to Trusted Social Work Authority

World War II interrupted John B. Turner's undergraduate education at Morehouse College. He enlisted and served as a First Lieutenant for the Tuskegee Airmen. After the war, he completed his bachelor's degree, then enrolled in the School of Applied Social Sciences to pursue graduate studies in social work, earning his Master of Science in Social Administration in 1948. Turner returned to Atlanta as an instructor at Atlanta University in 1950, then joined the Welfare Federation in Cleveland in 1952, where he became Director of Field Services.

While working for the Welfare Federation, Turner returned to the School to pursue his Doctorate in Social Welfare (DSW). He was appointed to the faculty in 1957 and earned his DSW in 1959. In 10 years, he would rise from Instructor to Professor and ultimately be appointed Dean in 1968—a position he held until 1973. He also was elected City Commissioner in East Cleveland and was a consultant to the National Urban League from 1966 to 1971.

Turner was highly prolific and internationally engaged. In 1971, he was a Short Term American Grantee of the U.S. State Department in Zambia, Ethiopia, Kenya, and Uganda. He served as consultant in an international research program in Cairo from 1972 to 1975, then returned to Egypt in 1977 to be Visiting Professor at the University of Minia. He participated in the International Council on Social Welfare as a member of the U.S. Committee, which he chaired for two years, and was a charter member of the International Association of Applied Social Scientists. Numerous published articles and books are to his credit, including Editor-in-Chief of the two-volume *Encyclopedia of Social Work* in 1977.

In 1981, Turner was appointed Dean of the School of Social Work at the University of North Carolina at Chapel Hill, where he served until his retirement in 1992 and was involved as Professor Emeritus until his death in 2009.

+ Dean John B. Turner.

ALUMNI PROFILE:
Margaret Brodkin, MSSA 1967

Founder and Director of Funding the Next Generation in San Francisco, Brodkin is one of the nation's pioneers in child advocacy. She is responsible for the passage and reauthorization of San Francisco's Children's Fund, bringing $750 million in new funding to children's services since its passage in 1991. Funding the Next Generation promotes local, dedicated funding streams in cities and counties throughout California. The project has engaged hundreds of activists, providers, and political leaders from dozens of communities.

From 1978 to 2004, she served as the Executive Director of San Francisco's Coleman Advocates for Children and Youth, successfully fighting for reforms in juvenile justice, youth development, early care, homeless services, health and child welfare, as well as the creation of a city department of children's services.

Brodkin was appointed Director of the San Francisco Department of Children, Youth, and Their Families in 2004, where she developed innovative models for coordination and standards of care, as well as a city policy for afterschool-for-all.

She headed New Day for Learning, a public/private partnership to promote community schools until 2012, when the project was integrated into the San Francisco Unified School District. Brodkin currently runs her own consulting firm working with public and non-profit agencies to create community change.

+ Margaret Brodkin,
MSSA 1967.

Guard. The next autumn, Carl B. Stokes was elected mayor of Cleveland, the first African-American mayor of a major American city. His victory was fueled by voters who felt the city needed new leadership that would focus on improving the most impoverished and run-down neighborhoods, and would actively manage the relationship between black neighborhoods and the largely white police force.

Stokes almost immediately turned to SASS for assistance, appointing Dean Stein to head the Commission on the Crisis in Welfare in Cleveland, with the purpose of addressing the city's growing poverty, particularly in its majority black neighborhoods. Stokes also turned to the Welfare Federation, the Cleveland Foundation, and other community organizations to create a $1.5 billion investment fund called Cleveland: Now! The fund was intended to revitalize the city by providing local grants to individuals and organizations to improve their own neighborhoods. One recipient of these funds was Ahmed Evans, a veteran and member of a black militant group, who sought to refurbish a storefront and create an African cultural center. In July 1968, Evans was involved in a shoot-out in Glenville with police that resulted in three dead officers, four dead citizens, and the second major riot in Cleveland within two years.

In the aftermath of the Glenville Riots, Louis H. Masotti, a political science professor and director of Case Western Reserve's Civil Violence Center, was awarded a federal grant to study the events. However, controversy erupted when the federal President's Commission on the Causes and Prevention of Violence delayed release of the final report, *Shoot-Out in Cleveland: Black Militants and the Police*, stating they did not wish to interfere with Evans' murder trial. Local activists objected, including the Students for a Democratic Society group at Case Western Reserve.

A series of protests erupted on campus in May 1969, when students and local black activists feared that the government was suppressing information that could have been used in Evans' defense. The protesters shut down a speech Masotti was intending to give, held rallies, occupied Adelbert Hall, and presented Case Western Reserve President Robert W. Morse and Provost Stein with a list of demands, including that the University use its influence to have the report released, shut down the Civil Violence Center, and secure Evans a new trial. President Morse responded by securing a restraining order against the protesters, which led a group of faculty members to issue *A Faculty Statement to the Campus Community*, defending the students' rights to peaceful protest and free speech and the university's role as a forum for the free exchange of ideas.

"We, as members of the faculty of the University, recognize our responsibility to involve ourselves more fully with the problems raised by recent events... The university must function as an open forum for the advocacy and examination of all ideas. Members of the university community must be free to promote social progress in accordance with their own judgement. We regard as totally unacceptable any resort to force, violence, or coercion as a means for the advocacy of ideas.... We call on all students to concern themselves with the issues of the day ... and to draw on the intellectual resources of the university in their efforts to understand such issues. We call on the faculty to address themselves to those issues and to the concerns of their students, and to aid in the development of a sense of community, by participating actively with the students in their efforts to confront such issues."

Among the 208 faculty members who signed the statement, 18 were from SASS, including Assistant Dean Marjorie Main, MSSA 1954; Director of Field Work Ruth Werner; and faculty members Art Blum, BA 1950, MSSA 1952; Susan Brubaker; Jack Joelson; Mary Reese; Kathryn Weitzel, MSSA 1941; Pearl Whitman; Margaret Hartford; Irving Rosow; and Gloria Donadella.

Provost Stein acted as an intermediary between activist students and faculty and the more conservative administration, going on campus radio station WRUW and appearing at an all-campus meeting to explain President Morse's point of view and take questions. Stein was viewed as a trusted go-between, something that has been cited as a significant factor in keeping protests peaceful at

+ Students rally and speak in front of Haydn Hall in support of Ahmed Evans, May 1969.

+ Three students at a continuing education program, 1969.

of turmoil. SASS was highly engaged with the endemic poverty, civil rights, welfare rights, and issues surrounding violence that the City of Cleveland faced. Looking within, the students, faculty, staff, and alumni examined their own approach to social work and to community engagement.

Shortly after King's assassination, students frustrated with the social work profession's failure to take political stands on social issues formed Student Involvement Now (SIN). The group's first act was to fundraise for the Southern Christian Leadership Conference and the Poor People's Campaign. They also held forums on community decision-making, professionalism and the urban crisis, the role of white social workers in black communities, and the politicization of the social worker. At around the same time, the School became the national headquarters of the National Federation of Student Social Workers, which had 89 member schools. The Federation worked to lobby national social work organizations regarding student participation and membership. Students were also involved in local protests, political campaigns, and with both the national and local Welfare Rights Organization and the Social Welfare Workers Movement.

Throughout these events, SASS remained nationally prominent in the social work profession. In 1969, the School co-hosted the Annual Program

Case Western Reserve. It was a role that would continue during the anti-Vietnam War protests and student strike of the early 1970s.

Outreach and Activism

At the same time, what had been a minor engagement overseas to protect the South Vietnamese against Soviet encroachment in the North expanded into what became the Vietnam War. Domestically, antiwar and civil rights demonstrations sparked more confrontations between police and protesters. Prominent national leaders such as Martin Luther King Jr. and Robert F. Kennedy were assassinated in 1968, further adding to the sense

Meeting of the Council on Social Work Education (CSWE) with The Ohio State University School of Social Work. Held in Cleveland, the meeting included Provost Stein, who was completing his third year as CSWE president, and Dean Turner, who served as chairman of the Ohio General Committee. That same year, Stein was also elected President of the Association of International Schools of Social Work.

Alumni Engagement

The School continued its own outreach to the social work community through a continuing education program, which offered classes for participants in the Cleveland International Program and held a popular annual series of Summer Institutes. Demand for the Institutes increased throughout the decade; by 1967, they offered sixteen separate summer classes. The Alumni Association created a Sunday Discussion Series in 1969 that featured presentations on current trends in social welfare. The first of these featured faculty member Marvin Rosenberg, PhD 1968, MSSA 1962, and alumna Steven Minter, MSSA 1963, then director of the Cuyahoga County Welfare Department. The Alumni Association also continued its work in bringing together local and national alumni through annual meetings held each year at the National Conference on Social Welfare, an Alumni Education Day,

+ Margaret Allen Ireland Library in Beaumont Hall.

an active National Advisory Board, and an annual telethon that raised money for scholarships.

As the 1960s drew to a close, the School celebrated smaller milestones in Beaumont Hall, such as the 1964 dedication of the Margaret Allen Ireland Library (named for the former Public Welfare Director for the State of Ohio and a longtime mem-

ber of the School's Advisory and Visiting Committees), the renovation of the student lounge, and the creation of new office spaces in 1966-67. By the mid-1960s, however, it was clear that SASS was facing a similar situation to what it faced in the Great Depression—the demand for professionally trained social workers to address the needs of a rapidly changing society was exceeding supply. In 1966, the School was even forced to end its application period early, as the number of applications received was the largest in its history. By 1969, 230 master's and doctoral students were enrolled.

In order to meet this increased demand, faculty began to make significant changes to curriculum, teaching, and research. By 1967, they had redesigned the doctoral program around three concentrations: research, teaching and research, and methods, social welfare policy and administrative practice. Beginning in 1969, the faculty created committees to discuss needed changes to the master's curriculum, consulting with the National Association of Social Workers, alumni, other departments at Case Western Reserve, the Visiting Committee, and community agencies. The committees included a faculty-student curriculum committee on which six students served and, more informally, the students and faculty held a series of "think-ins" throughout the year to discuss curriculum and operations.

To further enhance its approach to research, the School established the innovative Human Services Design Laboratory (HSDL) in 1969. HSDL was "created to provide problem-solving, research and demonstration-oriented assistance in developing new and more effective patterns of social work service." Early projects under HSDL's auspices focused strongly on addressing the needs of those living in poverty, including access to family planning, services for those with disabilities, securing employment, and fostering community development.

As it marked its 50-year milestone, the School's commitment to meeting the needs of its students, the social work profession, and the wider community helped guide it through the turbulent 1960s. Faculty, students, and alumni continued to speak out, conduct research, listen to their constituencies, and adapt to evolving social and cultural conditions—all of which would be essential in the 1970s and beyond. +

+ Students socializing in Beaumont Hall student lounge.

CELEBRATING 50 YEARS OF SASS IN 1966

In 1966, the School celebrated its 50th anniversary with an academic convocation, scholarly symposium, and awards dinner that attracted more than 1,000 people to one or more events, including representatives from schools of social work from around the nation, local scholars and community leaders, and international luminaries.

The academic convocation was held in Amasa Stone Chapel and featured an address by the Honorable Abba Eban, Israel's Minister of Foreign Affairs. At the convocation, Western Reserve University awarded honorary degrees to Abba Eban and to Philip Bernstein, MSSA 1934, who was the

+ Michael Harrington addresses the 50th Anniversary colloquium on September 30, 1966.

Executive Director of the Council of Jewish Federations and Welfare Funds in New York.

The symposium's theme was "Social Theory and Social Invention: The Translation of Ideas and Knowledge into Action for the Welfare of Society." Scholarly papers were presented by Gunnar Myrdal of Sweden; the Honorable Charles Frankel, a philosopher who was serving as the Assistant Secretary of State for Education and

+ Morton L. Mandel (lower left) at the 50th Anniversary Symposium.

Cultural Affairs; Michael Harrington, author of *The Other Americans*; and Melvin M. Tumin, a sociologist from Princeton University.

The symposium's panels, one of which was moderated by community leader Morton L. Mandel, included representatives from Yugoslavia, England, France, Columbia University, the University of Chicago, Brandeis University, the United Nations Bureau of Social Affairs, the National Urban League, and the federal government.

In an epilogue to Thomas F. Campbell's 1967 history of the School, Dean Herman Stein commented that the symposium attendees debated the role that social theory contributed to social invention. Stein noted, however, that everyone agreed that it was "mandatory that schools such as the School of Applied Social Sciences become increasingly involved in helping shape the course of human affairs." Stein ultimately saw the School as "reaffirming and recasting in today's terms the hope of the School's founders, who wished to organize a professional school wherein the social sciences would be drawn upon for direct application to the needs of society and community affairs."

The celebratory dinner was sponsored by the Alumni Association at the Sheraton-Cleveland Hotel, where Western Reserve University President John S. Millis presented special award citations to a group of distinguished alumni. The highlight of the night was when current and former deans performed "High SASS-iety: A Fifty Year Review of the School of Applied Social Sciences Done with Troubadours and Assorted Deans Live and In Color on Our Stage," a humorous look back at the School's history.

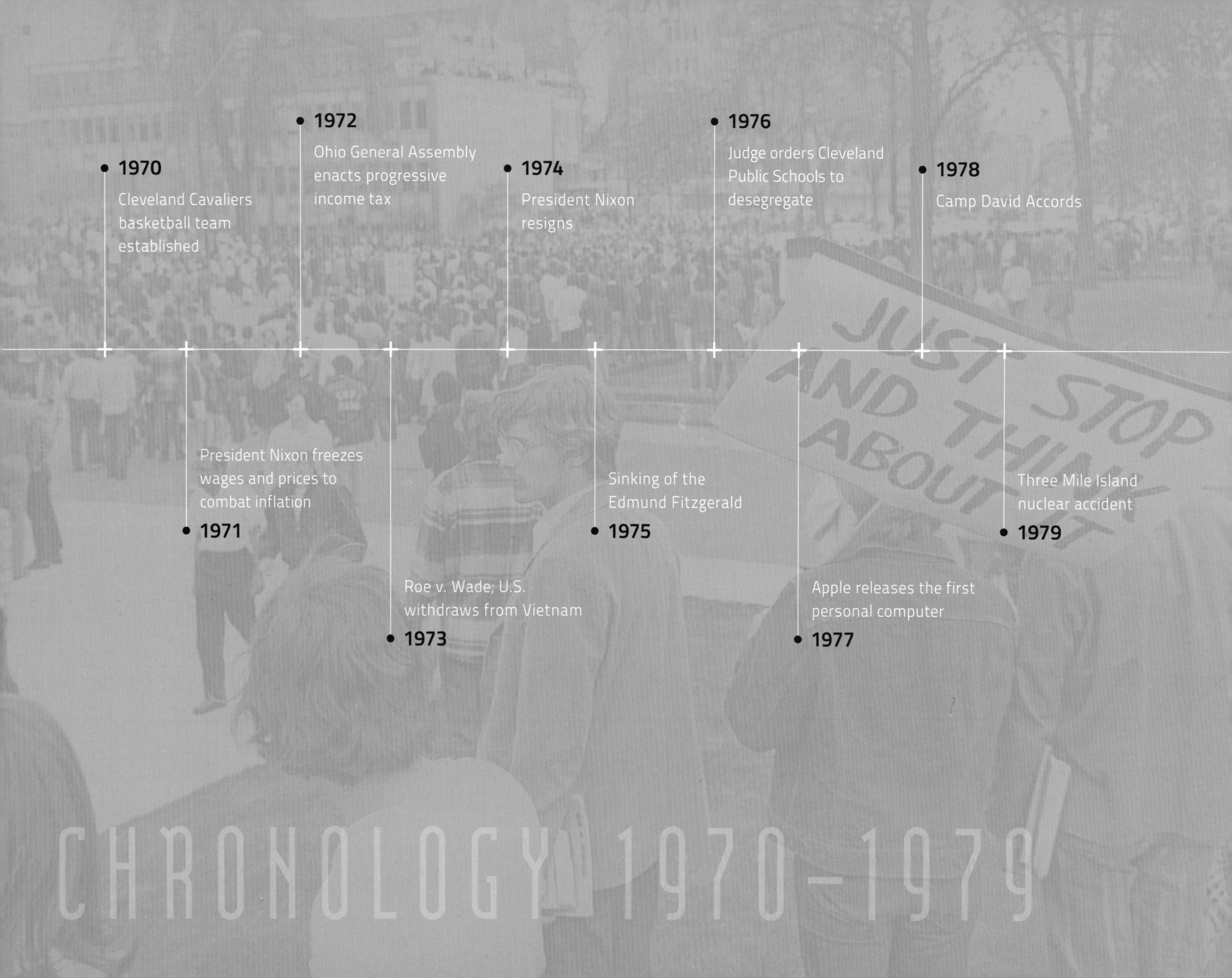

1970

Cleveland Cavaliers basketball team established

1971

President Nixon freezes wages and prices to combat inflation

1972

Ohio General Assembly enacts progressive income tax

1973

Roe v. Wade; U.S. withdraws from Vietnam

1974

President Nixon resigns

1975

Sinking of the Edmund Fitzgerald

1976

Judge orders Cleveland Public Schools to desegregate

1977

Apple releases the first personal computer

1978

Camp David Accords

1979

Three Mile Island nuclear accident

CHRONOLOGY 1970—1979

CHAPTER 6

Growth in Cleveland and Around the World

The tumult of the 1960s did not end with the start of a new decade. On April 30, 1970, President Richard Nixon announced that American troops would invade Cambodia alongside South Vietnamese troops, and protests on a national scale broke out against what was seen as an escalation of the war in Vietnam.

At Case Western Reserve, several thousand students and community members gathered for a rally against the war at noon on Monday, May 4. At the same time, similar rallies were taking place on college campuses across the country, including Kent State University, where the National Guard had been called out to quell large anti-war protests over the weekend. At 12:24 p.m., the National Guard opened fire on protesting students at Kent State. Four college students were killed. When

news of the deaths reached the Case Western Reserve campus, the protesters moved to block traffic on Euclid Avenue. Disbursed by a charge of mounted police officers, the students reconvened that evening for a vigil honoring those killed at Kent State.

The Students Strike

By the next day, Case Western Reserve students had declared a strike, refusing to participate in classes and instead organizing additional activism. After a lengthy faculty meeting broadcast live on campus radio station WRUW, President Morse announced that graduate and undergraduate students would have the option to either leave campus immediately and take their existing course grades (or a pass/fail), or remain on campus and complete their studies.

SASS students participated in the strike and raised a solidarity banner over Beaumont Hall. They joined with faculty to take immediate action. According to student Susan Green, they were "leafleting at shopping centers, schools, churches, factories; arranging a mass meeting of social workers at the [Jewish Community Center]; writing letters by the minute to senators in Washington." They also set up a crisis center to counsel students feeling overwhelmed and to give them space to "rap" with each other. In a speech at the Church of the Covenant given by student Joanna Davies on May 10, she explained what stood out to her in the days since the strike:

First: The feeling of unanimity between students and faculty, and the solidifying

65

+ Case Western Reserve students protest the Vietnam War in 1970.

of trust and faith in the competence and motivation of each other. Second: The repetitious theme in every meeting about the necessity for peaceful resolution of this crisis.... Third: I see the channeling of tremendous positive energy of students who may be free from the classroom, but have not elected to free themselves from the discipline of the hard physical and intellectual demands of their endeavor.

Green wrote in the Summer 1970 issue of the alumni newsletter that most of the people she had spoken with about the protests and subsequent student strike "were struck by the feeling of cooperation and solidarity between students and faculty at SASS." The nature of study at the School, which involved both classroom learning and field placements deeply embedded in the community, created opportunities for students to understand that the anti-war protests were taking place within the context of ongoing struggles for racial equality, economic opportunity, and conflict over education and welfare programs. African-Ameri-

+ Case Western Reserve student speaking to protest group.

THE ALCOHOL AND OTHER DRUG ABUSE (AODA) SPECIALIZATION

In 1976, SASS was the first social work school to establish a curriculum specialization in alcohol and other drugs (AODA) and since then has received more than $16 million in federal, state and local foundation grants to train thousands of social work students, licensed professionals, and faculty members.

It began in the early 1970s with funding from the National Institute of Alcohol Abuse and Alcoholism (NIAAA) for a training program for students and social workers "for effective direct practice with individuals and families experiencing problems with alcoholism, as well as planning, development, organization and administration of alcoholism programs." The Alcoholism Training Program, led by director Juanita Dalton, initially took place among a six-agency consortium of organizations that provided field training to students and instruction by community practitioners.

Dean Hokenstad recognized a need to better prepare students in the area of alcohol abuse and alcoholism, and he recruited and hired Lenore Kola in 1975. She assumed leadership of the program, added courses on alcoholism to the curricula, and developed the AODA specialization, focusing on interventions at both the micro and macro levels. She also developed a federally-funded AODA research training program for the school's doctoral program in 1977.

Over the years, Kola, Paul Abels, and others helped SASS remain at the forefront of substance abuse treatment. Throughout the 1980s and 1990s, they created new field placement offerings, added coursework to the doctoral and continuing education programs, and tested curriculum for NIAAA. In the early 1990s, Kola worked with

more than 30 other social work educators to create the Alcohol, Tobacco and Other Drugs (ATOD) Faculty Development program and "section." The National Association of Social Workers granted the ATOD section official status and appointed Kola to serve as its first chair.

In the late 1990s, the Woodruff Foundation asked Kola to create a training program around integrated dual disorder treatment for community practitioners. This led to a fellowship training program for students funded by the then Ohio Department of Mental Health, which in turn requested that SASS and the Department of Psychiatry in the School of Medicine develop the Substance Abuse Coordinating Center of Excellence in 1999—known today as the Center for Evidence-Based Practices.

+ Lenore A. Kola.

can students, although generally supportive of the strike and anti-war sentiment, were disheartened by the lack of national outrage over the shooting of student protesters at the South Carolina State University in Orangeburg in February 1970 during a protest against racial discrimination that left 27 students wounded and three dead.

Ambitious Recruitment and Curriculum Redesign

Despite the turmoil nationally and on campus, the School implemented a new series of recruitment strategies to reach prospective students across the country, particularly targeting undergraduate schools and national conferences. Joe Burrucker was hired in 1970 as the School's first financial aid coordinator and the first African-American participant in student recruitment efforts. Burrucker engaged current students and alumni in those efforts, writing that potential recruits were much more receptive to the idea of SASS once they had "the opportunity to 'rap' with graduate students." Burrucker spearheaded outreach to students from historically black colleges and universities, emphasizing the importance of having current minority students or alumni accompany him: "Visible confirmation on the student level, as well as some opportunity for undergrads to hear their rationale for coming to graduate school, with some recognition of comparisons of backgrounds, would prove immeasurably more effective than a solo effort."

Under the leadership of Dean Turner, the School embarked on an ambitious reorganization of the curriculum. After several years of faculty review, a detailed description of the new curriculum was put in place for the fall semester in 1970 which divided the course of study into three concentrations: Health, Socialization and Human Development, and Poverty and Community Development.

During the mid-1970s, curriculum adjustments continued. In the master's program, the School began to move away from the three concentrations and toward a series of specializations. Students continued to take the same core introductory classes in the first semester, but now chose a specialization in their second semester. The specializations were Aging, Alcoholism, Community and Neighborhood Development, Criminal Justice and Corrections, The Family and the Child, Federations, Health, Low Income Groups, Maternal and Child Health, Mental Health, Public Welfare, Social Work and the Schools. The focus on specializations allowed students more flexibility in designing a course of study, and allowed students to complete classes in multi-

ple specializations. The doctoral program strived to improve the diversity of its student population and continued to emphasize the program's focus on research on social policy and human service programs, particularly through the Human Services Design Laboratory (HSDL).

In 1973, Dean Turner stepped down. Interim Dean Ruby Pernell stepped in to run the School as a nationwide search was conducted for a new leader. That person was found the following year, when M.C. "Terry" Hokenstad—who had been Herman Stein's student at Columbia University School of Social Work—was appointed as Dean in 1974.

America's bicentennial in 1976 was a busy year at SASS. The Distinguished Service Award was established, honoring its first two recipients, Henry L.

+ Dean Hokenstad meets with community members.

After a 20-year career at the University of Minnesota School of Social Work, Ruby Pernell joined the faculty in 1968 and was appointed Interim Dean in 1973-1974. She was the Grace Longwell Coyle Professor in Social Work until her retirement in 1982 and had significant impact on group work education.

However, her renown is for her expertise in international social work, in particular as a social welfare attache to India for the State Department in the early 1960s, working closely with Ambassador Chester Bowles. Pernell is one of only two social welfare attaches in American history.

After completing her master's degree at the University of Pittsburgh School of Social Work and earning her doctorate at the London School of Economics, Pernell was hired by the University of Minnesota as a professor of social work in 1948 and is believed to be one of the first two black faculty members hired by a state flagship university in the 20th century.

+ Interim Dean Ruby Pernell in 1981.

Dean, 1974–1983 | NASW Social Work Pioneer
M.C. "TERRY" HOKENSTAD, PhD
Compassion Fuels Peerless Career in Social Work

M.C. "Terry" Hokenstad, Distinguished University Professor Emeritus and Ralph S. and Dorothy P. Schmitt Professor Emeritus, is a social work pioneer whose influence on research, education and policy extends far beyond the campus of Case Western Reserve University, where he's served students, colleagues, and the field for 44 years.

After a brief pursuit of the Episcopal ministry in England, Hokenstad chose a life in social work—a path "secular rather than sacred," he said, but still motivated by service to others. A move to New York City in the early 1960s proved pivotal. He marched in the streets during the Civil Rights Movement, earned a master's degree at Columbia University, and helped mobilize support for Medicare, the Older Americans Act, and other progressive legislation.

After earning a PhD at Brandeis University and becoming the first director of a then-new social work school at Western Michigan University, Hokenstad was recruited to become Dean of SASS in 1974. Under his leadership, the School recruited faculty members such as Claudia Coulton, PhD 1978, and Sharon Milligan and developed curricula around gerontology, AODA, health and human services management, and occupational social services. He also initiated joint degree programs with law, management, medicine, and nursing. During the 1970s, he worked with Congressman Louis Stokes to develop the Washington Semester program and was chair of the Mandel School's doctoral program from 1989–1994.

Perhaps the most enduring aspect of Hokenstad's legacy is his dedication to the international exchange of social work knowledge—from helping establish social work education in former countries of the Soviet Union, to training social workers in a rapidly aging China, to divining lessons from European social services for U.S. programs.

Today, he is a world-renowned expert in international social work, education, and aging who consults to the United Nations. Hokenstad has won countless social work awards and has written nine books on social work practice, education, elder care, and comparative social welfare, as well as serving as editor-in-chief of *The International Social Work Journal.*

+ Dean M.C. "Terry" Hokenstad in 1973.

Zucker, MSSA 1935, and Arthur H. Kruse, MSSA 1942; the *Journal of Applied Social Sciences* was founded and edited by Marvin Rosenberg, PhD 1968, MSSA 1962; and the School hosted the National Association of Social Workers regional conference.

Marking 60 Years of SASS

The 60th anniversary of the School was commemorated with a conference at Beaumont Hall on May 12-13, 1977. The theme "Cleveland's Human Services: Re-Examination of a Pioneering Community" emphasized the future of social work in the next decade. As faculty member Roger Ritvo noted in an alumni newsletter, the theme was especially relevant to the School's history, as "Cleveland's human and social services have been an integral part of the school's educational program through the years. Our graduates have assumed important roles in this community. The strong SASS-Cleveland relationship is not only a dominant trait of the past, but a goal of our future."

The conference presentations, which were ultimately published as a brochure, focused on leadership in the public and voluntary sectors, the future of social services, neighborhood and cultural pluralism, community-wide planning, social service personnel, the future of health services, and the role of public and private funding. The Alumni Association also held its annual meeting at the conference.

+ John Yankey teaches a class.

+ James Norton, the Chancellor of the Ohio Board of Regents, addresses 60th Anniversary Conference in 1977.

By the late 1970s, field education opportunities extended far beyond Northeast Ohio with the creation of the Washington Semester program, designed by Dean Hokenstad and the faculty to strengthen national outreach and provide students with the chance to study how social policy was developed and implemented on the federal level. Students did field work in the U.S. Senate and U.S. House of Representatives, including with Ohio Congressman Louis Stokes.

While SASS had focused on international social work for decades—working with the Cleveland International Program (CIP) and providing study opportunities abroad to students with the introduction of the Jamaica Program in 1972—the School increased its international activity during the late 1970s under the leadership of Dean Hokenstad. Faculty and students conducted research projects into the ways other nations approached social services and established new exchange programs. Visiting scholars came from England and from Sweden, and Dean Hokenstad and Roger Ritvo visited Sweden and Denmark, respectively.

The School also expanded its interdisciplinary focus, creating joint courses with other Case Western Reserve departments, including gerontological research and labor relations. The first student graduated from the joint MSSA/JD program with the School of Law, and plans were made to continue and expand these dual degree programs across campus.

Other notable events during the late 1970s included the creation of a new chair at the School, the Leonard W. Mayo Professorship in Family and Child Welfare, in 1977-78. While there had been other chairs created earlier, the Mayo Chair was the first to be fully endowed. With funding from the Eaton Corporation, SASS also added a new specialization in Federated Planning and Fund Raising, and the Cleveland Foundation funded construction of a new wing for Beaumont Hall.

The Human Services Design Lab (HSDL) conducted a national survey on behalf of YWCA regarding the organization's goal setting for the future. Led by Associate Dean Thomas Holland, HSDL also co-sponsored a conference in 1977 with the National Institutes of Mental Health on the topic of New Directions in Mental Health Research. In 1978, HSDL received a grant from the federal Department of Health, Education and Welfare to develop new curricula on direct practice in child welfare. The same year, Assistant Professor Richard Isralowitz became the new director of HSDL.

In August 1978, in lieu of the first day of classes, the School held a conference and workshop for its students on the topic of school desegregation, just as the City of Cleveland was about to begin the desegregation process. Faculty designed the conference to help students see how desegregation may affect their field work and how social work agencies could play a role in the process. Participants included Case Western Reserve faculty, representatives from the YMCA and the Greater Cleveland Project, and representatives from Cleveland's law department.

The School continued to focus on providing information to both the general public and social work practitioners on the latest developments in the field and on contemporary social issues. In 1976, SASS held a Public Information Colloquium Series with sessions on child abuse and alcoholism. The continuing education program flourished during the late 1970s, providing courses on income maintenance, working with children and families, coping with violence, the role of self-help groups, labor relations and management, and programs for field instructors on practice models and group decision making. Faculty member Edmond T. Jen-

kins, MSSA 1966, also provided a course on "Innovative Techniques with Individuals, Families, and Groups," which demonstrated then brand-new therapeutic practices such as echoing, mirroring, and doubling.

Student and Alumni Collaboration

The Alumni Association continued its yearly telethon to raise scholarship money, as well as organizing regional alumni committees and helping to plan the 60th anniversary conference. It developed a close working relationship with the Student Association, asking student representatives to serve on alumni committees, co-sponsoring events, and helping to establish a committee on job placement. Alumni helped sponsor various events, including a Homecoming potluck held at the Shaker Lakes in 1977, a disco-themed dance to welcome students and faculty in the fall of 1978, and a yearly "Beer Blast" that featured music and dancing.

The Student Association was very active. They created a new newsletter, "Student Stream," in September 1976, which provided news, events, and allowed students and faculty to publish poetry, drawings, and short stories. Student organizations raised money for scholarships, created orientation events for first-year students, and hosted the National Federation of Student Social Workers in November 1976.

+ Alumni in continuing education class.

Students lobbied the faculty and administration for more flexible options for coursework and field placements, asked for the inclusion of material on racism and sexism in their classes, and requested more sections of introductory courses, as the number of students entering the MSSA program increased during the late 1970s. With the increase in enrollment also came an increase in student field placements: in 1978 there were 326 students placed with 132 agencies across Northeast Ohio and in Washington, D.C. and the Jamaica Program.

A new student organization, Hermanos en Unidad Latina, was founded in 1976 to make students aware of bilingual cultures and Latin American issues. That same year, SASS students joined Case Western Reserve students from the Schools of Medicine, Dentistry, Nursing, Library Science,

+ Students socializing in the student lounge.

The Margaret Allen Ireland Library said goodbye to longtime librarian Martha Stewart, who retired in 1977 after serving five deans. The library continued to embrace the latest technology, creating a Multi-Media Lab in 1976 that featured a collection of videotaped casework material to be used in classes, as well as two video cameras and three audiocassette recorders. The Library purchased a new Xerox copy machine in 1976, one of the few coin-operated Xerox 3100 models made in the United States.

The 1970s were characterized by growth—expansion in the student population and the School's geographic and racial diversity, increasing collaboration with other departments in the University, ongoing cooperation with community agencies, innovation in the field through initiatives like the Human Services Design Lab and the Cleveland International Program, and a willingness for students and faculty to confront controversial contemporary issues—from the anti-war movement to desegregation to supporting research that would benefit marginalized people coping with chronic mental health and addiction problems. +

and the Departments of Psychology and Podiatry to form the Student Health Coalition (SHC), which worked to improve communication between these departments and schools, because they often worked with the same patient populations. The Association of Black Student Social Workers (ABSSW), founded in 1958 as the first organization formed for African-American social workers in Cleveland, helped sponsor a student conference on desegregation, provided tutoring and book loan services, conducted voter registration drives, created a Big Brother/Big Sister program pairing African-American second year students and first year students, and hosted a Halloween party and soul food dinner.

ALUMNI PROFILE:
Maureen Dee, MSSA 1978

Cleveland is a long way from Montevideo, Uruguay, which is where Maureen Dee was born and raised. At 18, she moved to the United States for college. After practicing bilingual social work in New York City, she was recruited by the School of Applied Social Sciences and has made Cleveland her home ever since. Today, Dee is Executive Director of Treatment, Prevention, and Recovery Programs at Catholic Charities Corporation in the Diocese of Cleveland, where she manages behavioral health programs in Cuyahoga County.

Founder of the Hispanic Alliance, Dee started several juvenile justice programs to address the use of alcohol and other drugs among at-risk teens and has served on the Ohio Recovery Council, the Ohio Chemical Dependency Credentialing Board, and the Cuyahoga County Service Coordination Team under Families and Children First Council. She is an active board member of the Hispanic Roundtable, Latina, Inc., Scarborough House, and the MetroHealth System. Dee is a member of the School's Visiting Committee and is a mentor for the Leadership Fellowship Program.

+ Maureen Dee, MSSA 1978, with Leadership Fellow mentee Kaitlyn Uhl, MSSA 2016.

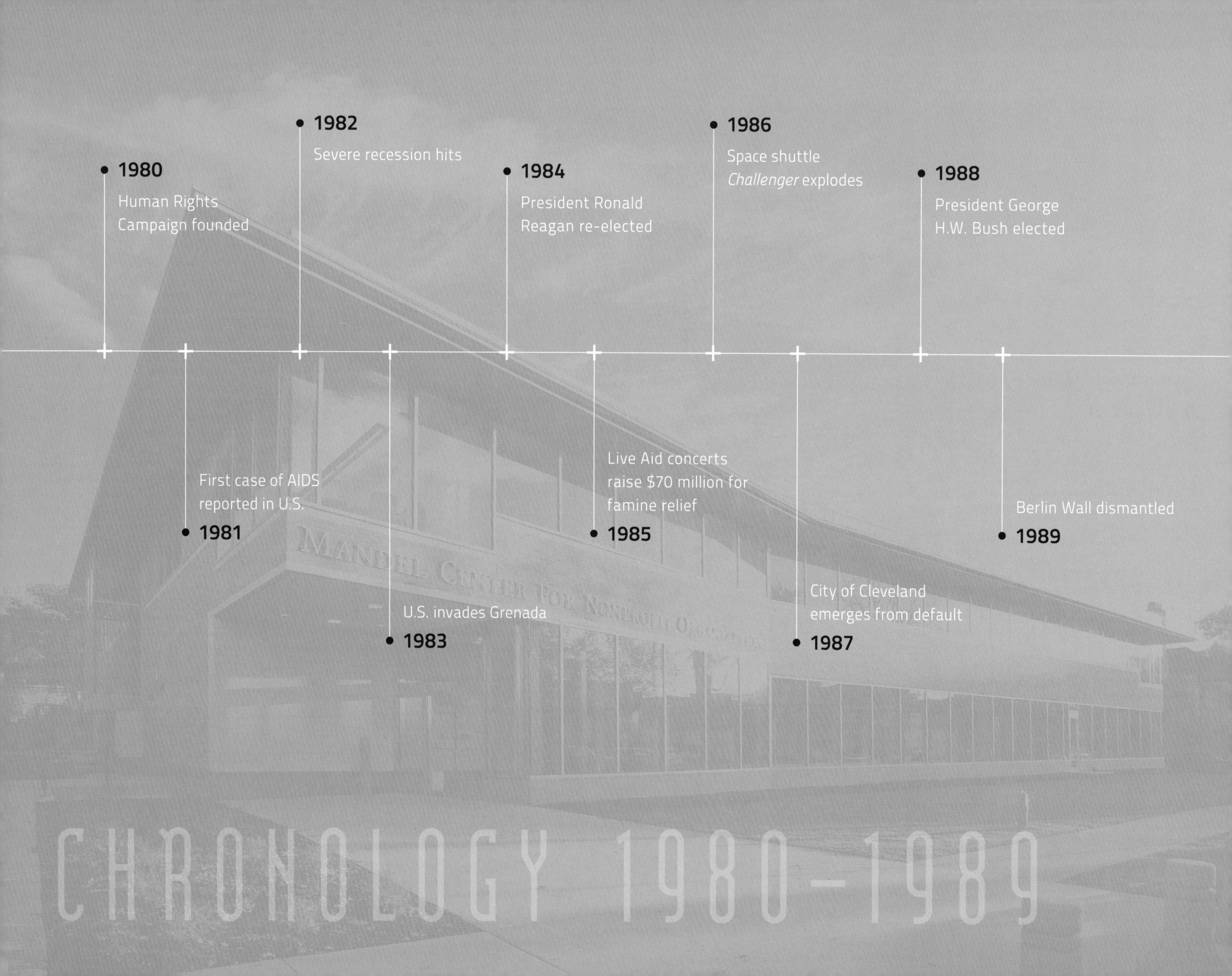

1980

1982
Severe recession hits

1984
President Ronald
Reagan re-elected

1986
Space shuttle
Challenger explodes

1988
President George
H.W. Bush elected

1980
Human Rights
Campaign founded

First case of AIDS
reported in U.S.
1981

Live Aid concerts
raise $70 million for
famine relief
1985

Berlin Wall dismantled
1989

U.S. invades Grenada
1983

City of Cleveland
emerges from default
1987

CHRONOLOGY 1980-1989

CHAPTER 7

Groundwork for the Future

The 1980s were a transformational time for the School of Applied Social Sciences. It entered the decade ranked as one of the top five American schools of social work by *The Gourman Report,* alongside the University of Chicago, Co-

+ Joseph, Jack and Morton L. Mandel at the 1988 convocation with their copies of the Board of Trustees' resolution renaming the Mandel School of Applied Social Sciences.

lumbia University, University of Michigan, and the University of California at Berkeley. At the same time, its location in Cleveland had become a challenge, as the city coped with the results of its financial default in 1978, the turmoil of school desegregation, and ongoing disinvestment in public housing and poor neighborhoods.

However, the School's vital role as an institution of research, teaching, and social service innovation embedded in the city made it a launching pad for new approaches to community engagement as well as creative solutions for maximizing local, national, and international impact in an environment of scarce resources—especially as federal funding for social services decreased, causing money shortages for agencies and social workers.

Philanthropists Jack, Joseph and Morton L. Mandel recognized the vital role of the School to make lasting social change at the intersection of social work research, education, practice, and community collaboration. In 1988, the brothers decided to make a major investment in it by giving $3 million—the biggest gift in the School's history—to support construction of a new school building and ongoing programs. Their donation resulted in a new outlook, a new future, and a new name: The Mandel School of Applied Social Sciences.

Long-Range Leadership

Under Dean Hokenstad and Associate Dean John Yankey (who also served as Acting Dean in 1980-81), the Mandel School worked to implement a

Interim Dean, 1980–1981
JOHN YANKEY, PhD
A Strategic Asset to Nonprofit Management and Social Work

Currently the Leonard W. Mayo Professor Emeritus in Family and Child Welfare and co-chair of the Mandel School's Centennial, John Yankey continues to teach courses in strategic planning and developing strategic public and nonprofit partnerships. During his 43 years at the School, Yankey has administered a number of statewide leadership training programs with public child welfare and human services agencies in Ohio, as well as served in a variety of administrative functions for the Mandel School, Mandel Center for Nonprofit Organizations, and Case Western Reserve.

Throughout his career, Yankey has written articles and books that have been used to teach nonprofit management and social service administration across the United States. His work on fundraising, creating strategic alliances, board governance, and social service management includes co-editing *Skills for Effective Management of Nonprofit Organizations*, material disseminated nationally by BoardSource, and an article, "Strategic Alliances," which is included in the Jossey-Bass *Handbook of Nonprofit Leadership and Management*.

Yankey earned his undergraduate degree from Alderson-Broaddus College in West Virginia, his MSW from West Virginia University, and his PhD from the University of Pittsburgh. Prior to joining to the faculty, Dean Yankey worked in the West Virginia Department of Human Services, rising to become the agency's Chief Operating Officer. In that capacity, he also coordinated the state's intra-governmental relationships, public-private partnerships, and strategic planning.

Even more than his writing, Yankey's presence in the classroom and work as a consultant with hundreds of community organizations has demonstrated his commitment to creating change in the ways that nonprofit and social service organizations do business. Yankey has won many awards for teaching, social work, and executive leadership, including "Distinguished Mountaineer" by his home state of West Virginia and "Social Worker of the Year" by the state of Ohio. He has also been selected as "Teacher of the Year" multiple times by students at the School.

+ Interim Dean John Yankey in 1977.

new Long-Range Plan that called for innovative approaches to social welfare, the building of new relationships with the community, and a renewed focus on research and collaboration.

In 1983, Hokenstad stepped down as Dean, but continued to serve on the faculty as the Ralph S. and Dorothy P. Schmitt Professor of Social Work, an endowed chair created in 1980 in honor of civic activist and philanthropist Dorothy Prentiss Schmitt, the first chairwoman of the Visiting Committee. His successor was Arthur Naparstek from the School of Public Administration at the University of Southern California, who also became the Grace Longwell Coyle Professor in Social Work. Dean Naparstek retired in 1988 to become President of the Premier Industrial Foundation and Mandel Associated Foundations. He was succeeded by Richard L. Edwards, the Acting Dean of the School of Social Welfare at SUNY Albany.

The groundbreaking for the new building took place on October 26, 1989, placing the Mandel School at the vanguard of a new era for Case Western Reserve. It was a key player in the growth of the University under Presidents David V. Ragone and Agnar Pytte and the Mandel School building was the first constructed under the University's new Master Building Plan.

Student Recruitment Plan

Federal reductions to student financial aid led to a decrease in enrollment in the master's degree program. In response, the School created a Student Recruitment Plan to boost out-of-state enrollment in partnership with the Alumni Association. The majority of students during the early 1980s were Northeast Ohioans over the age of 25 who already worked for a social service agency and held an outside job to help pay tuition. Enrollment in the master's program would increase significantly throughout the decade due to the Extended Degree and Intensive Semester programs, which allowed students to complete their degrees over a longer time frame, as well as through classes held during evenings, weekends, and over the summer.

After the success of the Intensive Semester, the Mandel School added more flexible coursework options for the doctoral program, allowing students to complete intensive classes over the summer or in January. A new joint Master's/PhD program in 1986–87 provided students the opportunity to complete both degrees within four years. In response to the underrepresentation of minorities in research and academic positions in the social work field, the doctoral program renewed its focus on minority recruitment.

Dean, 1983–1988
ARTHUR J. NAPARSTEK, PhD
An Imaginative Public Policy Thinker

Dean from 1983 to 1988 and the Grace Longwell Coyle Professor in Social Work from 1991 until his death in 2004, Arthur J. Naparstek was an expert on urban redevelopment and neighborhood revitalization whose community-building concepts served as the basis for local and national government programs in both the United States and Israel.

As Dean, the Mandel Center for Nonprofit Organizations and the Center on Urban Poverty and Community Development were founded, as well as the Intensive Weekend social work master's program. Senator Barbara Mikulski worked with Naparstek and Congressman Louis Stokes on housing legislation, a collaboration she described as an "iron triangle," of which "Art was the brain trust."

Naparstek's work helped redefine the function of public housing through community-building. As director of the Cleveland Foundation Commission on Poverty in the early 1990s, he oversaw the drafting of The Cleveland Community-Building Initiative report, which became the foundation for the U.S. Department of Housing and Urban Development's Urban Revitalization Demonstration Act of 1993, known as HOPE VI. U.S. In 1994, Naparstek was appointed to the Corporation for National Service by President Bill Clinton.

The co-author of four books on community-building and mental health in public policy, Naparstek also applied his community building skills to improve the economic base and sense of community in Beit She'an, a city in northern Israel; resolved longstanding conflicts between Ashkenazi and Sephardic Jewish communities; orchestrated a meeting between the mayor of Beit She'an and the Palestinian governor of Jenin which served as a model for Israeli Prime Minister Ehud Barak in 11 other towns throughout Israel.

At his funeral in 2004, Mikulski called Naparstek "one of our most imaginative public policy thinkers." In 2005, the Mandel Center for Nonprofit Organizations established the Arthur J. Naparstek Philanthropic Fund based on gifts totaling nearly $1.6 million, which endows two scholarships per year. His papers can be found at the Western Reserve Historical Society in Cleveland.

+ Dean Arthur Naparstek.

EDUCATIONAL ACCESSIBILITY: Intensive, Extended, and Online Degree Programs

Throughout its history, the Mandel School has renewed its commitment to educational innovation and accessibility with the continual creation of programs that meet the needs of students—even someone who will never set a foot on campus—putting a top-ranked professional graduate school education within reach of more people who want to help people.

Extended Degree Program

In the 1980s, the Extended Degree program allowed students to complete their program during a three-year period (with academic work the first year and a combination of academic and field work in the second and third years).

Intensive Semester (Now Called Intensive Weekend)

The Intensive Semester (later called Intensive Weekend) program was designed for already-employed social workers, allowing students to complete a master's degree over a five-year period. Starting in 1989-90, the Intensive Semester option was also offered in the doctoral program for several years, with PhD students completing coursework over three summers and two "January periods," or over two summers and an academic year. Today, the Intensive Weekend program attracts master's students from throughout Ohio and the Midwest for classes one weekend per month for Direct Practice students specializing in AODA, Children Youth and Families, or Mental Health (Adults).

Online MSSA Program

In 2013, the Mandel School launched Case Western Reserve's first fully-online graduate degree program. "The Online MSSA offer the unique opportunity to receive a rigorous graduate education from a top social work school without the need to relocate," said Dean Gilmore. Online students take master's courses customized and taught for them by the same faculty in the on-campus program, and they can do their field work at their workplace or an agency near their home. In 2016, nearly half the MSSA students enrolled at the Mandel School were online.

Streams Merged and Direct Practice Program Established

As part of the mission to train students to provide leadership at the cutting edge of social work practice, faculty continued to make adjustments to the curriculum. In 1982, they introduced a program in industrial social work, which trained social workers to assist employees in factories and the workplace rather than an agency setting.

In 1987, they merged the "B Stream" (Planning, Development, and Organization) and "C Stream" (Human Service Management) course tracks into a new stream called Planning, Development, and Management.

The faculty also made a significant change with the establishment of the Direct Practice program, which was designed to create new and innovative ways of social practice in the community through curriculum creation, continuing education programs, and research. It linked faculty and students with agencies and community partners to create programs that addressed systemic needs in the community. Direct Practice became a major initiative and new faculty were hired to expand the program, including Kathleen J. Farkas, PhD 1984; Mark Singer, PhD 1983, MSSA 1979; and Elizabeth Tracy.

The faculty added electives and field placements in education, learning and development, juvenile justice and corrections, public welfare, and community development. The specializations were also reduced to five: Aging, AODA, The Family and the Child, Health, and Mental Health.

The Henry L. Zucker Professor of Social Work was created by Morton L. Mandel and other friends of Zucker in 1985 in honor of Zucker's career as a social worker and the 50th anniversary of his graduation. The chair also became a part of the Direct Practice program, with David Biegel hired as the Henry L. Zucker Professor of Social Work in 1987.

The Mandel School built a foundation for its future in the 1980s by investing in many of the initiatives and centers that are still prominent today, including the Mandel Center for Nonprofit Organizations and the Center on Urban Poverty and Social Change.

+ Students and faculty in 1982.

ALUMNI PROFILE:
Georgia Jean Anetzberger, PhD 1986, MSSA 1980

Georgia Jean Anetzberger has been active in the field of aging for more than 40 years as a planner, administrator, researcher, educator and consultant with a focus on elder abuse. She has conducted pioneering research and authored more than 70 scholarly publications, including the books *The Etiology of Elder Abuse by Adult Offspring* and *The Clinical Management of Elder Abuse*.

Anetzberger was founder of the Ohio Coalition for Adult Protective Services, president of the National Committee for the Prevention of Elder Abuse, and editor of the *Journal of Elder Abuse & Neglect*. She helped establish the oldest state and local elder abuse networks in the United States, was the architect of Ohio's adult protective services law, and served on numerous national and state panels to elevate elder abuse research, policy, and practice. She has held executive management positions at the Benjamin Rose Institute and Western Reserve Area Agency on Aging, as well as faculty positions at Cleveland State University and Case Western Reserve University.

A Fellow of the Gerontological Society of America, Anetzberger has received numerous awards for her accomplishments, including being inducted into the Ohio Senior Citizens Hall of Fame in 2013. She is a member of the Mandel School Visiting Committee.

+ Georgia Jean Anetzberger, MSSA 1980, PhD 1986.

MANDEL CENTER FOR NONPROFIT ORGANIZATIONS FOUNDED

In March 1984, a University partnership of the Mandel School of Applied Social Sciences, the Weatherhead School of Management, and the School of Law established the Mandel Center for Nonprofit Organizations, created to fulfill its mis- sion to strengthen the leadership and management of nonprofit organizations and made possible by the vision and support of the Mandel brothers.

In collaboration with the Cleveland Foundation, the George Gund Foundation, and the Sohio Philanthropic Pro- gram, Henry L. Zucker, MSSA 1935, of the Mandel broth- ers' Premier Industrial Philanthropic Fund approached the University about housing the center, which initially provided continuing education for nonprofit executives and supported faculty research through grants from the Mandel Research Scholars program. The Mandel School contributed faculty and courses to the Center's newly cre- ated Certificate in Nonprofit Management (CNM), which welcomed its first class of 26 students in 1987.

"The need for leaders who possess the talent and commitment required to change the world has never been greater, and we are pleased to collaborate with Case Western Reserve University as it enhances academic offerings for people dedicated to making a meaningful difference for others," said Morton L. Mandel.

In its formative years, the Mandel Cen- ter was directed by Arthur Blum, DSW 1960, MSSA 1952, then Richard P. Chait. In 1988, Dennis R. Young was appointed director. He was a Professor and Director of Nonprofit Studies at the W. Averell Harriman College of Policy Analysis and Public Management at SUNY Stony Brook, as well as a visiting faculty member at the Yale University In- stitute for Social and Policy Studies' Pro- gram on Nonprofit Organizations.

Young helped launch the Master of Non- profit Organizations (MNO), which was ap- proved by the Ohio Board of Regents in 1989 and was one of the first two nonprofit grad- uate programs offered in the United States. The first MNO classes were held in Septem- ber 1989 with an enrollment of 31 students.

The Mandel Center also began publish- ing a journal, *Nonprofit Management and Leadership*, in conjunction with the Center for Voluntary Organisation at the London

School of Economics. Executive education and management training programs continued to expand. The Mandel Center hosted a Distinguished Public Lecture Series and Discussion Paper Series to draw attention to research on the state of the nonprofit sector. During the 1990s, the Mandel Center sponsored national research conferences, collaborated with the School of Law to implement a Nonprofit Law Clinic to provide legal services to local nonprofit groups, and worked with the George Gund Foundation to create a Nonprofit Management and Governance Clinic. Nationally, the Mandel Center played a leading role in the formation of the Nonprofit

Academic Centers Council in 1991, with Young serving as its founding chairman.

In 1995, the Mandel Center for Nonprofit Organizations celebrated its 10th anniversary by moving to a new space on Euclid Avenue in the Hearing and Speech Center Building, commissioning a history, and hosting a research conference. It also established a national Think Tank with funding from the Lilly Foundation, which for several years brought 20 chief executives and 10 academics together for three days to discuss nonprofit management issues. In 1998, it was the recipient of a four-year, $800,000 grant from the W.K. Kellogg Foundation for community service projects, a review of the CNM and the MNO curriculum, and a study of whether or not undergraduate and doctoral programs were feasible for development.

In 2007, the Mandel Center moved into a new building located on Bellflower Road on campus. The two-story, 11 million dollar building was financed with a generous $6.75 million donation from the Jack, Joseph and Morton Mandel Foundation and the Mandel Supporting Foundations. Designed by Kallmann, McKinnell & Wood Architects, Inc. in collaboration with Case Western Reserve's Office of Campus Planning, the building features a lecture hall, meeting and classrooms, offices, lounges, as well as a rooftop garden and courtyard. The 25,000 square foot building allowed the Mandel Center's programs and staff to be under one roof.

One of the first nonprofit leadership programs in the country, by 2010 the Mandel Center for Nonprofit Organizations faced competition from more than 300 institutions offering nonprofit management education. In April 2012, after a two-year review of programs under interim director Richard Boyatzis, Case Western Reserve and the Mandel Foundation agreed that the best path forward was to restructure the program to ensure

quality nonprofit education in the future. The MNO and CNM are now offered by the Mandel School, and Weatherhead offers an Executive MBA Nonprofit Certificate, with classes taken at both Weatherhead and the Mandel School. The Mandel Center building was renamed the Jack, Joseph, and Morton Mandel Community Studies Center and now houses two Mandel School research centers, in addition to classroom and meeting space.

MANDEL CENTER DIRECTORS AND ACTING DIRECTORS

Arthur Blum

Richard P. Chait

Dennis R. Young

John Palmer Smith

John Yankey

Susan Lajoie Eagan

Richard Boyatzis

+ Dennis R. Young in 1987.

+ Faculty members with 10 or more years of tenure in 1988.

State and Local Outreach

In accordance with its mission statement, the School continued its policy of creating partnerships and collaborative projects with multiple state and local agencies. The School provided consulting services, project evaluation, training, and student field placements to local agencies. Among these were:

- The Cuyahoga County Income Maintenance Department: Assisting the Cuyahoga County Department of Human Services to shift its welfare and food stamp programs from a "case bank" to a "case load" system in 1985, which allowed individuals receiving assistance to work with the same caseworker for both

programs. It proved so successful that it received multi-year funding and students were given field placements to assist county workers with the project. By 1987, the School secured funding to help workers from Cuyahoga and Summit counties to enter the master's degree program.

- Child Welfare Management Project: A partnership with the Ohio Department of Public Welfare (OPPW) to provide continuing education courses to sixteen agencies in the OPPW's Cleveland District with funding from federal Title XX funds and the Cleveland Foundation. With funding from the federal Department of Health and Human Services, the School created the Child Welfare Project in 1982 to provide assistance to families and social workers in meeting the needs of children, which consisted of student field placements, dedicated coursework, workshops, and the creation of a manual and instructional tape.

- Cleveland Public Schools: A collaboration with the Center for Corporate Involvement in the Cleveland Public Schools to establish the Cleveland Partnership. One outcome was the Career Beginnings Program at John Adams, East, and Shaw High Schools, created with funding

from the Edna McConnell Clark Foundation. It paired students with "teacher brokers" and ministers from the Inner-City Renewal Society who served as mentors. Students were also given career training, summer job placements, and college preparation advice.

- Ohio Executive Institute: Created as a joint venture with Cleveland State University's College of Urban Affairs and the Ohio Department of Administrative Services to provide leadership training for 50 state officials, including members of the Governor's cabinet. The School also created the Ohio Family and Children Services Executive Training Institute to conduct management training for the executives of Ohio's state and county human service departments and children's services boards.

In the National Spotlight

Students, faculty, and staff continued to be well-represented nationally:

- Service to national organizations: Dean Edwards was elected president of the National Association of Social Workers in 1989.

- Assisting federal agencies: In 1980-81, Assistant Dean Roger Ritvo was appointed a Government Fellow by the American Council of Education and worked on health policy analysis in the office of Secretary for Health

THE CENTER ON URBAN POVERTY AND COMMUNITY DEVELOPMENT:
Innovating the Use of Big Data for Major Social Change

In 1988, the Rockefeller Foundation and Cleveland Foundation provided the Mandel School with funding to conduct an analysis of poverty in the city of Cleveland. To administer this process, the Rockefeller Foundation agreed to assist the School and the Cleveland Foundation in creating the Center for Urban Poverty and Social Change (or Poverty Center)—one of six centers established nationally, but the only one based in a university.

Led by co-founding directors Claudia J. Coulton, PhD 1978, and Regina Nixon, the Poverty Center's first task was to create a database of statistical indicators of individuals living in poverty in Cleveland from 1979 to 1988, tracking poverty, access to government programs, infant mortality, pregnancy rates, access to housing, property values, education level, and employment. This data became the basis for a report on poverty conditions in Cleveland neighborhoods that would eventually prompt the formation of a citywide commission and the passage of major federal legislation in urban development.

In 1993, the Center on Community Development was founded and led by Arthur Naparstek and Angela Lowder of the Mandel School. Along with the Poverty Center, it was instrumental in helping a five-square mile part of the city of Cleveland win federal designation as an "urban empowerment zone" in 1994, which allowed the city to secure $100 million in federal aid and tax incentives for neighborhood development. In 2006, the Center on Community Development merged with the Poverty Center, leading to the creation of the current Center on Urban Poverty and Community Development.

The Poverty Center has never stopped updating its data on poverty statistics in Cleveland neighborhoods. Now called NEO CANDO, the Northeast Ohio Community and Neighborhood Data for Organizing is a free and publicly accessible social and economic data system that contains longitudinal and census data from 1980 to the present on Cleveland and 17 counties that comprise Northeast Ohio. It has been used by researchers around the world.

In 1999, it created the ChildHood Integrated Longitudinal Data (CHILD) System, which collected data from 20 nonprofit and governmental sources on children in Cuyahoga County since 1992 and supports the Poverty Center's evaluation of multiple programs, including Pre-4Cle, which works to ensure that all children in Cleveland have access to high-quality preschool; MomsFirst, a home visiting and case management program run by Cleveland's Department of Health to address racial disparities in infant mortality rates; and Pay For Success, which works to reduce foster care stays for children from homeless families.

Today, the Poverty Center continues to use research and data innovations to strengthen families and communities. It supports the East Cleveland Partnership—which brings together local government, residents, nonprofits, and the faith community to revitalize East Cleveland—and is the home of the National Initiative on Mixed Income Communities, created in 2013 (see Chapter 10). The Poverty Center's current co-directors are Coulton and Robert Fischer.

+ Regina Nixon and Claudia Coulton upon co-founding the Poverty Center.

and Human Services in Washington, D.C. That same year, with funding from the federal Community Services Administration, the School partnered with the School of Law to created "Project Fair Play," which worked to improve the administration of the federal Aid to Families with Dependent Children program. Under project director Alvin L. Schorr, the program studied AFDC in five states to identify problems that families encountered while applying to the program.

Case Western Reserve University professors Jerome Liebman, left, Robert L. Dickman, Sharon Milligan and Alvin L. Schorr support a national health care plan.

Profs see demand for federal care

By META McMILLIAN 3-21-88
STAFF WRITER

The growing number of poor and medically uninsured Americans soon will demand that the chaotic manner in which physicians provide care be replaced by a national health plan to provide more uniform quality care.

That is the consensus of a group of Case Western Reserve University professors of medicine and social work who spoke last night at a health care forum at the Thwing Center on campus.

Dr. Jerome Liebman, professor of pediatrics at the CWRU medical school, said that one of the biggest problems with the present medical care system was lack of accessible care for the poor and those in the low middle income bracket.

He also cited a big maldistribution problem, meaning that citizens in areas like Eastern Tennessee and Kentucky get less medical care because of their distance from medical centers.

"Right now, health care is in chaos," he said. "We won't see change tomorrow, but there will be a move in a few years."

Liebman said he believed the nation would move more toward a national health insurance plan like that used in Canada. Under such a plan, each state would adopt its own medical system, which would be subsidized by the federal government and taxes.

Liebman and his associates, Drs. Robert L. Dickman and Amasa B. Ford of the medical school and Sharon Milligan and Alvin L. Schorr of the CWRU School of Applied Social Sciences, co-authored an article in the New England Journal of Medicine. All but Ford appeared last night.

Dickman, professor of family medicine, said there was no way to measure quality care under the present free enterprise system. "We have got free enterprise, corporate medicine and it doesn't work. Medicine is not a commodity. You can't take people who deal with other people's lives and try to treat it like buying airline tickets."

The group estimateed that 37 million Americans have no health insurance at present.

The nation's present health care system is the result of reactions from the federal government, physicians and insurance companies to the health needs of citizens or their reaction to criticisms about the lack of health services, the CWRU group said.

None of these entities share a national vision of health care that the public can support and invest its resources, the group said.

Because there is no shared vision, attempts to change some health care systems that have been absorbed by the public, such as Medicaid, become difficult because of political obstacles, the authors wrote.

Liebman said the public needs to be better educated about national health plans so they can shed their fears about socialized medicine and fears about losing their right to choose a doctor. Americans equate socialized medicine with socialism, Schorr said.

The United States and South Africa are the only developed countries without a national health care plan, the professors said.

The CWRU group said present medical systems has made physicians more cautious about which services they provide and which patients they may treat. Physicians' concerns about paperwork and insurance coverage may cause some to shy away from some medical services.

Additionally, those problems physicians face may be causing them to shy away from private practice. The authors said the proportion of physicians in private practice has declined from 80% in 1931 to 68% in 1959 to 58% in 1980.

+ Faculty activism featured in *The Plain Dealer.*

- National visibility: In 1983, a study on ethics committees in hospitals conducted by faculty member Claudia Coulton, PhD 1978, Stuart Youngner from the department of psychiatry, and David L. Jackson from the School of Medicine for the Presidential Commission on Medical Ethics was featured in national broadcasts by both NBC and CBS News. In 1989, the *Journal of Applied Social Sciences*, based at the Mandel School and edited by Pranab Chatterjee, introduced a format redesign and recruited a national editorial advisory committee.

International Connections

The School expanded its international outreach during the 1980s. It hosted visiting scholars from Israel, Australia, and Norway and continued an exchange program with the Social Welfare Training Center at the University of Kingston in Jamaica begun by Ruby Pernell in 1972. Dean Hokenstad traveled extensively throughout the decade, visiting both Stockholm University in Sweden and the National Institute for Social Work in London during a sabbatical year to work on comparative research projects.

Close ties with Tel Aviv University in Israel were established via Art Blum, PhD 1960, MSSA 1952, who helped develop that school's social work curriculum, served on the faculty at both schools, and facilitated joint research projects between students.

Student and Alumni Engagement

Throughout the 1980s, the Student Association remained active and students participated in organizations such as the Women's Alliance and the Association of Black Student Social Workers. They continued to be vocal in advocating for improvements to the student experience, suggesting changes to existing coursework and evaluations, holding career workshops and student orientations, creating a phone hotline to provide support for stressed out students, and conducting self-defense classes.

The Alumni Association grew significantly with the addition of the doctoral graduates in 1986 (prior to this, doctoral graduates were considered part of the Graduate Studies alumni). They improved outreach with an expanded newsletter, now a magazine named *SASS Action*, still published today as *Action*. The Alumni Association founded its first chapter in Akron, held its first annual conference featuring former Dean Turner as the speaker, and created a career services office. In June 1987, the

Alumni Association hosted the first All-Alumni Reunion Weekend (the theme was "Convergence"), featuring three days of social events, continuing education, and get-togethers for alumni, students, and friends.

As the Mandel School ended the 1980s, it was poised to continue its growth with a new name, new programs, and a new building. Cleveland was beginning to restore its financial footing, construction revitalized downtown, and the city's service economy grew, although the problems of poverty, income disparities, poor public housing, and struggling public schools remained. The world was also changing with the fall of the Communist states, many of which would seek help from the West in creating modern social service agencies. The Mandel School was qualified to meet these problems head on, and would continue to change Cleveland, the United States, and the world during the 1990s. ✛

A NEW NAME AND A NEW HOME

A significant milestone in School history occurred on March 19, 1988, when the University Board of Trustees passed a resolution to rename it the Mandel School of Applied Social Sciences, in recognition of a $3 million gift from the Premier Industrial Philanthropic Fund for the construction of a new building and the creation of a permanent endowment fund—and, more significantly, the special and longtime relationship between the School and the Mandel brothers. At the time, the name change made it one of only seven named schools of social work in the United States.

By the 1980s, Beaumont Hall was more than 30 years old, showing its age and its inadequacy to keep pace with the School's growth. In 1989, plans were approved for a new building, located at the corner of Ford Drive and Bellflower Road. The 43,000-square-foot building was designed by Western Reserve University alumnus James Polshek of James Stewart Polshek and Partners to serve as "a people place" and to promote "a sense of openness and a spirit of communication" with its many meeting rooms and common areas. The building also included a computer facility with sixteen computers, fiber optic cable, and a media lab. Kicked off with the generous gift from the Mandel brothers, the fundraising campaign for the new building was successful. It included a $500,000 gift made by Lillian F. Harris, MSSA 1932, to the school library, which was renamed the Lillian F. and Milford J. Harris Library. The groundbreaking for the new building was held on October 26, 1989.

✛ Construction of the MSASS building, September 1989.

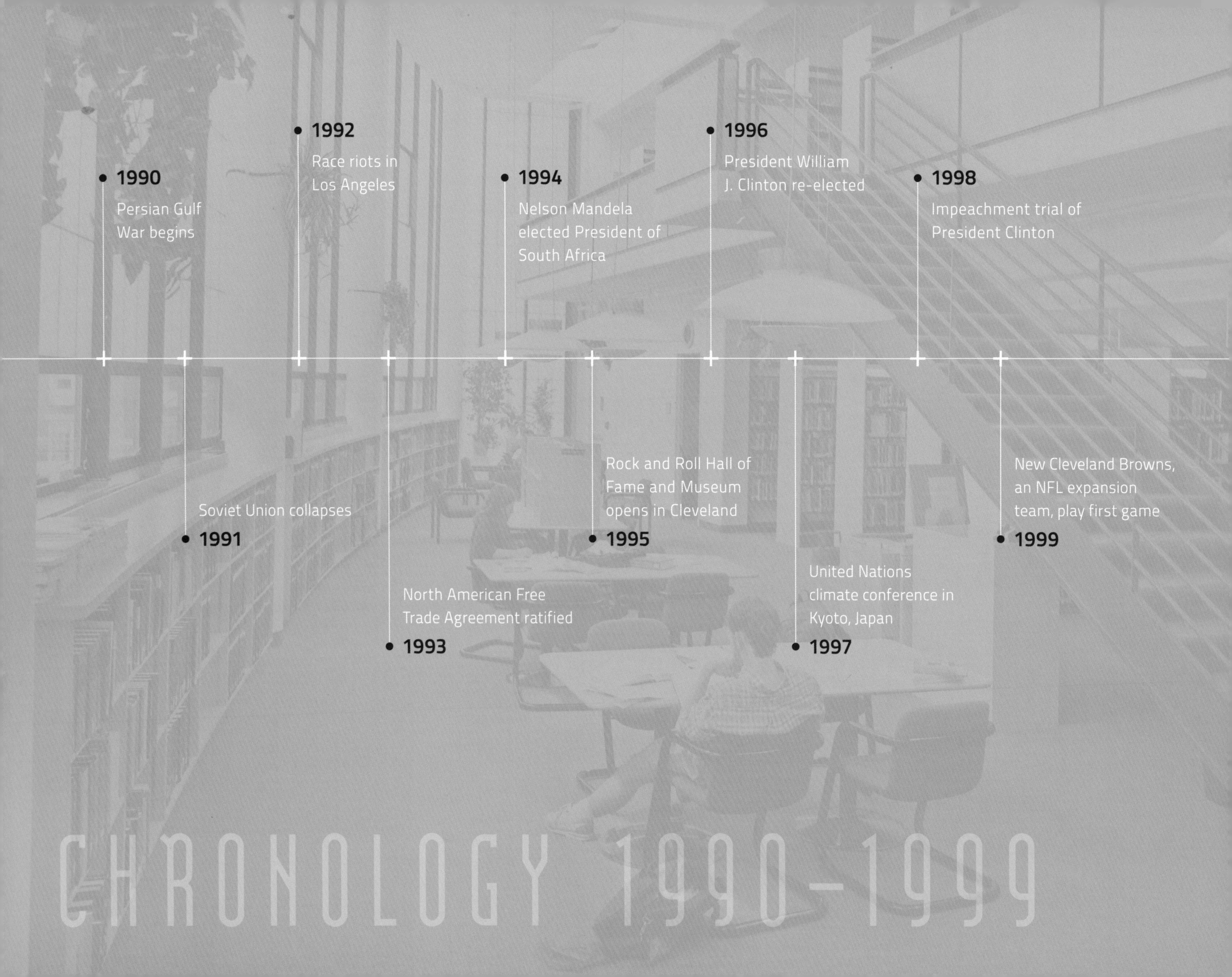

1990

Persian Gulf
War begins

1992

Race riots in
Los Angeles

1994

Nelson Mandela
elected President of
South Africa

1996

President William
J. Clinton re-elected

1998

Impeachment trial of
President Clinton

Soviet Union collapses

1991

North American Free
Trade Agreement ratified

1993

Rock and Roll Hall of
Fame and Museum
opens in Cleveland

1995

United Nations
climate conference in
Kyoto, Japan

1997

New Cleveland Browns,
an NFL expansion
team, play first game

1999

CHRONOLOGY 1990-1999

CHAPTER 8

Visionary Transformation

The Mandel School of Applied Social Sciences entered the 1990s at the forefront of a wave of transformation that swept through Cleveland and the Case Western Reserve campus. The Gateway project, the Rock and Roll Hall of Fame, the Great Lakes Science Center, and a revitalized entertainment district changed the face of downtown, while the new Mandel School building became the first project built under the University's Master Building Plan.

A New Home

Classes were first held in the new school building on January 3, 1991. Thanks to the generosity of the Jack, Joseph and Morton Mandel Foundation and other donors, it boasted double the number of classrooms than had been in Beaumont Hall,

multiple meeting spaces and offices, and was the first building on campus fully wired for network and security-card access. James Stewart Polshek and Partners, the building's architects, were awarded the American Institute of Architects' 1992 Firm of the Year Award, and the building was featured prominently in the issue of *Architecture* magazine announcing the award. The formal dedication of the building took place on May 13, 1991, with more than 800 guests in attendance. There was also a ribbon-cutting ceremony held that day for the Lillian F. and Milford J. Harris Library, which contained more than 25,000 volumes in 6,800 square feet on two floors, along with a state of the art computer lab.

MSASS remained prominent both at home and nationally, with *U.S. News & World Report* ranking

+ The newly-built MSASS building.

+ Dedication of the MSASS building on May 13, 1991. From left to right: Morton, Joseph and Jack Mandel; Dean Richard L. Edwards; vic gelb (holding microphone).

MANDEL SCHOOL OF
APPLIED SOCIAL SCIENCES

Case Western Reserve University
1990

+ **Left:** Lillian F. Harris and Dean Richard L. Edwards in front of the Harris Library on August 22, 1991. **Right:** Case Western Reserve President Agnar Pytte, Jack Mandel, Morton Mandel, Dean Darlyne Bailey, Joseph Mandel, and Board of Trustees Chair John Lewis at a luncheon honoring the Mandel family on May 4, 1998.

the School 7th among graduate schools of social work in 1993–94, a ranking it maintained throughout the decade, and the School continued to serve as a site for national collaboration. In 1991, MSASS hosted the national conference of the Family Preservation Educators Working Group, which developed a new curricula for graduate schools of social work. The following year, it hosted meetings between representatives from twelve universities as they created the North Central Field Education Directors Consortium. And MSASS played a significant role in the 1996 National Association of Social Workers meeting, which was held in Cleveland.

It was also well-represented in national publications. In 1995, the 19th edition of *The Encyclopedia of Social Work* featured twenty contributions from faculty and alumni, reflecting the School's prominence in social work practice. In a 1996 survey by researchers at Virginia Commonwealth University, MSASS faculty ranked first among forty-five social work schools with doctoral programs for having the most articles published in social work journals per capita.

During the 1990s, the School renewed its mission and commitment to community building and creating partnerships, which was reflected in its

new mission statement, adopted in September 1994: "MSASS provides and integrates professional social work education, research and service to promote social justice and empowerment through social work practice in communities locally, nationally, and internationally."

Dean Edwards served the School until 1992, when he was appointed dean of the School of Social Work at the University of North Carolina, Chapel Hill, succeeding former dean John B. Turner, DSW 1959, MSSA 1948, in that position. Wallace Gingerich was interim dean from 1993–94, then Associate Professor Darlyne Bailey was appointed dean in July 1994.

JACK, JOSEPH AND MORTON MANDEL:
Investing in Future Leaders and Setting a Standard of Excellence

Jack, Joseph and Morton Mandel have transformed the School that bears their name with their generosity and steadfast commitment to creating leaders in social change.

"Mort and his brothers Joe and Jack have been visionary philanthropic leaders committed to making the world a better place. They have made an enormous difference in the development and success of our school. Their investments have allowed us to prepare future leaders, and their high standards of excellence always embolden us to reach greater heights," said Grover C. Gilmore, the Jack, Joseph and Morton Mandel Dean in Applied Social Sciences.

After co-founding Premier Industrial Corporation in 1940, they created the Jack, Joseph and Morton Mandel Foundation in 1953, one of the largest philanthropic foundations in the United States, to benefit people worldwide by supporting leadership education programs and socially relevant initiatives. Its priorities are leadership development, management of nonprofits, humanities, Jewish life, and urban renewal.

The Mandel brothers have been an integral part of Case Western Reserve for more than 50 years, from when Mort Mandel moderated the School's 50th anniversary conference panel in 1966, to when he was the first to earn the School's new minor in social work when he received his undergraduate degree in 2013 (74 years after putting his education on hold), to when he celebrated the Mandel School's Centennial with the current and former deans in 2016.

In 1984, the Mandel family helped endow and found the Mandel Center for Nonprofit Organizations, a cooperative venture between MSASS, the School of Law, and Weatherhead School of Management to offer advanced education for people who manage and govern human services, educational, arts, religious, and philanthropic organizations.

In 1988, the Mandel Foundation served as the lead donor for the construction of the School building on the corner of Ford and Bellflower, which is when SASS was renamed the Mandel School of Applied Social Sciences. In 2013, they were the lead donors of the capital campaign for the building renovation, with a $4.95 million gift that was part of an $8 million award that also endowed the dean's chair and changed the name of MSASS to the Jack, Joseph and Morton Mandel School of Applied Social Sciences. Along the way, they significantly funded student scholarships, strategic priorities, and were essential partners in the School's progress.

Joseph Mandel also gave the School a beloved piece of his own artwork. An avid sculptor, he created the brightly-colored modern metal sculpture in the back courtyard of the Mandel Community Studies Center, which he donated in 2007. He passed away in 2016 at the age of 102. Jack Mandel, the oldest brother, died in 2011 at the age of 99.

> *"The hallmark of our philanthropy is our commitment to invest in people with the values, ability and passion to change the world."*
>
> *—Jack, Joseph and Morton Mandel*

+ Joseph, Morton and Jack Mandel *(Nannette Bedway).*

+ Morton, Jack and Joseph Mandel at the groundbreaking for the
new MSASS building on October 26, 1989.

Dean, 1988–1992 | NASW Social Work Pioneer
RICHARD L. EDWARDS, PhD
Scholar, Administrator, and Innovative Leader

With a background in hospital and psychiatric social work, Richard L. Edwards became Dean of the Mandel School in 1988. Under Edwards' leadership, the school relocated from its former location at Beaumont Hall to a newly constructed building that is its current home on the corner of Bellflower and Ford roads.

At the same time, he also served as president of National Association of Social Workers (NASW). During his presidency, NASW introduced into Congress the first fully comprehensive and budgeted national health care reform that sparked the national debate and visibility of the issue.

Edwards is the author of numerous publications about the impact of social policy on service delivery, organizational effectiveness, and social work services in rural areas, and he was editor-in-chief of the 19th edition of the *Encyclopedia of Social Work*. He previously served as dean of the School of Social Work at the University of North Carolina, where he also served as interim provost. Edwards was appointed the dean of the School of Social Work at Rutgers University in 2005. He then served as interim president, interim chancellor, and executive vice president for academic affairs. He is currently the Chancellor at Rutgers University-New Brunswick.

"I think that social work education is great in terms of preparing people for all kinds of leadership roles, because whether you're going to become a manager, fundraiser, or executive in social work, you're going to learn about forming relationships," said Edwards in 2016.

+ Dean Richard L. Edwards in 1988.

Former Dean Arthur Naparstek was appointed the Grace Longwell Coyle Professor in Social Work in 1991, and John Yankey became the Leonard W. Mayo Chair in Family and Child Welfare the following year, a newly-created chair. In 1997-98, another new chair, the Lillian F. Harris Professor of Urban Research and Social Change, was created and attached to the Center for Urban Poverty and Social Change; Poverty Center founding co-director Claudia J. Coulton, PhD 1978, became the first Harris Professor. In 1999, after his retirement from Congress, the Honorable Louis Stokes joined the faculty as the Senior Visiting Scholar in the Practice of Social Policy and Community Revitalization.

Major Milestones

MSASS celebrated several significant milestones during the 1990s, beginning with its 75th anniversary in 1991-92. The festivities began in September with a concert given by community organizer and folk singer Si Kahn, and culminated the following April with a dinner and conference. The School also honored its 80th Anniversary in 1996-97 with several receptions and a workshop designed to assist social workers with changing technology. Other major events included the renewal of the School's accreditation with the Council on Social Work Education in 1993.

Celebrating 80 years

MSASS

MANDEL SCHOOL OF APPLIED SOCIAL SCIENCES

The Alumni Association set records for fundraising during the 1990s, regularly raising over $100,000 per year for the Annual Fund. The School also received the largest amount of private funding in its history in 1997-98, approximately $3.6 million. The Student Association partnered with alumni during the 1990s in a "match" program that paired students with alumni mentors with similar interests. The Alumni Association also worked closely with faculty and staff on a successful food drive for Harvest for Hunger in 1992 that raised 1,144 pounds of food and $1,200 in donations from a soup kitchen lunch, plant sale, bake sale, raffle, and waffle breakfast. The food drive also proved to be a good natured rivalry between students and the faculty and staff, with the latter winning with a last minute donation of a 100-pound bag of rice and twelve one-gallon cans of beans.

The Student Association continued to evolve throughout the decade, changing its structure in

Dean, 1994–2002
DARLYNE BAILEY, PhD
A Commitment to Multidisciplinary and Multicultural Practice

After earning a doctorate in organizational behavior from Case Western Reserve University, Darlyne Bailey worked as an administrator and a clinician in the mental health field, then began her academic administration career in 1994, when she was appointed Dean of the Mandel School.

During her tenure, she expanded the School's endowment and research funding, worked with the Mandel Foundation to establish the Mandel Fellows and Mandel Scholars, and invited Congressman Louis Stokes to join the faculty in 1998 upon his retirement from Congress. In 1995, she organized the first Midwestern Deans and Directors Conference at the Mandel School, which produced the "White Paper on Social Work Education—Today and Tomorrow."

Bailey's career has been founded on a commitment to multidisciplinary and multicultural practice. She has been the Principal Investigator for many studies around the country and was named one of the most influential African-American social workers by NASW. She has written numerous articles and also co-authored several books and handbooks including: *Strategic Alliances Among Health and Human Services Organizations: From Affiliations to Consolidations* and *Sustaining Our Spirits: Women Leaders Thriving for Today and Tomorrow.*

Bailey was born in Harlem, New York, and received her bachelor's degree from Lafayette College in Easton, Pennsylvania. She completed her master's degree from the Columbia University School of Social Work and attained her doctorate in organizational behavior from the Weatherhead School of Management at Case Western Reserve University. Today Bailey is at Bryn Mawr College, where she is Dean Emeritus of the Graduate School of Social Work and Special Assistant to the President for Community Partnerships.

+ Dean Darlyne Bailey in 1999.

CLAUDIA J. COULTON, PhD 1978
Distinguished University Professor
Inaugural Fellow, American Academy of
Social Work and Social Welfare

Alumna Claudia J. Coulton, PhD 1978, the Lillian F. Harris Professor of Urban Research and Social Change, is world-renowned for her visionary work using data to address society's most pressing problems. Inspired by her parents and the example of Martin Luther King Jr.'s Poor People's Campaign, Coulton chose a career in social work, earning a bachelor's degree in sociology from Ohio Wesleyan University in 1969 and a master's degree in social work from The Ohio State University in 1972. After spending several years working in Columbus, Ohio,

+ Claudia J. Coulton *(Steve Zorc)*.

Coulton pursued her doctorate in social welfare at the Mandel School.

Coulton joined the School's faculty in 1978 as an Assistant Professor. She became an Associate Professor in 1981, Professor in 1984, chair of the doctoral program, and Associate Dean for Research from 2003-2008.

In 1988, Coulton co-founded the Center on Urban Poverty and Social Change (now the Center on Urban Poverty and Community Development) with funding from the Rockefeller Foundation and the Cleveland Foundation. It pioneered the collection and use of "big data" to analyze the effects of poverty on Cleveland neighborhoods. Coulton was instrumental in the creation of NEO CANDO (NorthEast Ohio Community and Neighborhood Data for Organizing) in 1992, a publicly-accessible database of information on neighborhoods in northern Ohio. The database set a national standard for data collection and continues to be a significant community resource.

She is also the founder and Executive Committee Member of the National Neighborhoods Indicators Partnership (NNIP), a consortium of over 35 cities that uses data to understand the macro-level systemic forces that produce poverty, as well as the lead researcher for the Annie E. Casey Foundation's Making Connections research program and a research adviser to Cuyahoga County's Invest in Children Program.

Throughout her career, Coulton has been a dedicated researcher and teacher, having written over 150 articles, books, book chapters, and research reports. She is a nationally recognized expert on the foreclosure crisis and has testified before Congress. In recognition of her scholarship, teaching, research, and service, Case Western Reserve University named Coulton a Distinguished University Professor in 2012, and she was awarded an inaugural fellow of the American Academy of Social Work and Social Welfare in 2010.

1997–98. The new Student Coordinating Board now encompassed multiple student caucuses including the Diversity Roundtable, Local and International Konnections (LINK), the Intensive Weekend Caucus, the Black Student Association, and the Non-Traditional Student Caucus.

The Harris Library embraced computers and the Internet, adding a CD-ROM collection, World Wide Web access, the ability to receive and transmit articles via fax, and a laptop borrowing program for students. In 1994-95, the library created its first website and, with a donation from Lillian Harris, added an information technology center in 1995-96 that included projectors and new computers featuring Netscape and WordPerfect 6.1. By the decade's end, the Harris Library began piloting a program to use the Internet to deliver course materials to students in the Intensive Weekend program. In 1997-98, the School would further embrace technology with the creation of HomeNet, an information system developed with Cuyahoga Community College and other community partners that provided data, social supports, and credit advice to potential homeowners in Cleveland. (HomeNet would evolve into the HomeToday demonstration project during the 2000s.)

During the late 1980s and the early 1990s, the School embarked upon an intensive student recruitment campaign. While MSASS graduated the largest class in its history in May 1990, this was due largely to curriculum changes in the late 1980s that reduced the number of credits required to graduate, allowing a large number of students to complete the program that year. The School held open houses on campus and in Ohio, Pennsylvania, New York, and West Virginia, and sent faculty and staff on recruitment trips to schools and social service agencies. Throughout the early 1990s, the number of full-time students applying to the master's degree program increased and the school brought in an increasing amount of students from outside of Ohio and the United States. The School's Project GO program, which provided educational support to minority students, enrolled a record number of students (12) in 1991-92. By 1994-95, the School's total enrollment was at 533, then the largest in MSASS history. By the end of the decade, there were 423 students enrolled in the MSSA program, with half of those students enrolled full-time, 40% in the Intensive Weekend program, and the remainder in the Extended Degree program. There were 71 doctoral students.

Faculty continued to update the curriculum in response to the needs of its students and social work practitioners in the field. In 1991, a faculty and staff task force suggested dividing it into the "Foundation Curriculum" and the "Advanced

+ The Lillian F. and Milford J. Harris Library in July, 1994.

+ Sharon Milligan teaching a class in November, 1995.

+ Faculty members Kathleen Farkas, Neil Abell, and Elizabeth Tracy in 1995.

Curriculum." The Foundation Curriculum consisted of 15 credits from four core classes (social policy, social work methods, socio-behavioral theory, and research), plus a semester of field education and a skills lab. The Advanced Curriculum included 45 credits in six concentrations, plus four electives and three semesters of field education. Career tracks in fundraising (in partnership with the Mandel Center) and community development were also added for master's degree students in 1993.

Students in the doctoral program participated in a mentoring program which partnered students with faculty members one-on-one during the pre-dissertation stage, and students were encouraged to join the research programs of the various MSASS research centers. In 1997–98, the School and the Mandel Foundation created the Mandel Leadership Fellows Program, which recruited five doctoral students each year who had demonstrated leadership in the field of social welfare. Each student was assigned two mentors, one from the faculty and one from the student's field of interest. In 1998-99, the Grace F. Brody Institute of Parent-Child Studies was created, which provided scholarships to doctoral dissertations and studies related to parent-child interactions.

The end of the 1990s saw the creation of an Assessment Task Force to recommend changes to the master's degree program and to create learning outcomes. Faculty examined creating a "community practice framework" for the curriculum and identified what it called the "Eight Abilities," skills that competent social workers needed to develop in order to effectively practice in the field. These abilities would ultimately be incorporated into the Ability-Based Learning Environment (ABLE), which would reshape the Mandel School curriculum in the next decade (see Chapter 9).

The School also maintained its commitment to providing continuing education for social work practitioners, creating a Certificate Program in Clinical Social Work Practice in 1990. The first class had six participants. Continuing education also provided workshops and licensure review courses every year and expanded the sites for workshops to include the cities of Lorain, Westlake, Dayton, and Wheeling, West Virginia.

Research Centers and Community Partnerships

The School's research centers continued to grow throughout the decade, serving as places where faculty, staff, students, agencies, and funding sources could develop new initiatives, interact, and promote research. They became instrumental in the work of helping Cleveland address its continuing problems with poverty and struggling public schools, as well as providing resources for Ohio's human services and child welfare workers. The Mandel School also partnered with the Mandel Center for Nonprofit Organizations in providing training to executives and staff in the growing nonprofit sector.

ALUMNI PROFILE
Steven Minter, MSSA 1963

Steve Minter's impact can be seen in almost every part of Cleveland. From 1984 to 2003, Minter was President and Executive Director of the Cleveland Foundation, overseeing the organization's mission and growth in its assets and grant-making, which had far-reaching implications for an untold number of civic initiatives in Greater Cleveland, ranging from school reform and neighborhood develop-

+ Steve Minter, MSSA 1963.

ment to arts and culture and public health. "It's easier to say which things we shouldn't associate his name with," Diana Tittle, author of *Rebuilding Cleveland: The Cleveland Foundation and Its Evolving Urban Strategy* told *Crain's Cleveland Business* in 2010. "It would be hard to find any positive development of the last 25 years that he wasn't associated with in some way,"

Now the Executive-in-Residence and a Fellow in the Center for Nonprofit Policy & Practice at the Maxine Goodman Levin College of Urban Affairs at Cleveland State University, Minter also spent more than 15 years in governmental positions: Under Secretary for the United States Department of Education during President Carter's administration; Commissioner of Public Welfare for the Commonwealth of Massachusetts from 1970 to 1975; and between 1960 and 1970 (as he was pursuing his MSSA at the School), he rose through the ranks from caseworker to the Director of the Cuyahoga County Welfare (1969).

The centers allowed the Mandel School to assist the post-Cold War democracies that were building schools of social work and creating brand new human services and child welfare agencies. They also represented the School's embrace of technology, as the Poverty Center created databases that tracked poverty and neighborhood demographics, conducted studies on exposure to violence, and used fax machines and the Internet to share research more rapidly.

The School's Practice Demonstration Program became The Center for Practice Innovations (CPI) in July 1991, co-directed by David Biegel and Kathleen J. Farkas, PhD 1984, and was a university-community partnership between the School and local human service agencies to develop new models of delivering services to vulnerable populations. This was done through demonstration projects, information exchanges, training programs, and research. In its first year, CPI received funding from the George Gund Foundation, the Martha Holding Jennings Foundation, and the Premier Industrial Foundation, and 32 students participated in its projects. CPI continued its Jewish Communal Services Initiative and the Low-Income and Minority Initiatives, as well as its working paper series and Family Caregiving Project. New initiatives included assisting chemically dependent low-income women find access to social services through the Women's Re-entry Resource Network and helping to establish support networks for newly immigrated parents of children in Head Start programs. It produced an Occasional Paper Series, a ten-volume interdisciplinary book series called Family Caregiver Applications, and a series with Oxford University Press called Innovations in Practice and Service Delivery with Vulnerable Populations. New demonstration projects included using computers for case management, an investigation of the experiences of violence by inner city high school students, evaluating an assistance program to help families with HIV and drug-exposed children, conducting a study of the need for mental health support services in Erie County, and establishing social services centers at Cuyahoga County Metropolitan Housing Authority public housing sites staffed by students.

In 1993–94, the Center for Practice Innovations (CPI) established two major research institutes: the Cuyahoga County Community Mental Health Research Institute (CCCMHRI) and the Joseph C. and Florence Mandel Alzheimer's Disease Caregiving Institute.

CCCMHRI was a partnership with the Cuyahoga County Community Mental Health Board and was led by the Board's Jeffrey A. Johnsen and David E. Biegel and Kathleen Wells from MSASS to study children and adolescents with emotional disorders and adults with mental disabilities. It also hosted visiting researchers, held research forums, expanded its website, and supported postdoctoral students.

The Joseph C. and Florence Mandel Alzheimer's Disease Caregiving Institute, led by Baila Miller, worked with faculty from other Case Western Reserve schools and human service agencies to focus both on research and supporting caregivers. It completed a four-year study of how minorities used long-term care, provided internships through the Great Lakes Interdisciplinary Team Training Program, and created training materials.

CPI also established two awards for students who developed innovative field education programs to prevent child abuse (the Norma C. and Albert I. Geller Award for Child Abuse Prevention) and to assist the aging (the Julius and Helen Weil Award, later the Schnurmann Foundation Award). Funding shortages would lead to the closure of CPI in June 1997, but its research institutes, projects, and violence prevention program remained in operation.

The School's partnership with local school districts also continued throughout the 1990s, with the Professional Careers Center operating the Career Beginnings Program for students from the Cleveland, Euclid, and Warrensville Heights School Districts (the program became part of the Urban

BUILDING INTERNATIONAL RELATIONSHIPS AFTER THE COLD WAR

With the fall of Communist regimes throughout Europe in the early 1990s, the Mandel School became instrumental in addressing social work needs in the former Soviet Union and its satellite states. Over the course of the decade working with the federal government and private organizations, it established close relationships with universities and governments in central Europe, helping them to create social services and educational programs.

In March 1990, Dean Edwards and faculty member Alice K. Johnson visited Romania and began a collaborative project with Jim and Barbara Bascom of World Vision. Called STAIR (Services Training and Institutional Redesign Project), the project was designed to link programs that provided Romanian social workers with services training and curriculum development. With the assistance of the Cleveland International Program, groups of Hungarian and Romanian social workers visited the Mandel School each year, a program which continued throughout the decade.

Former Dean M.C. "Terry" Hokenstad developed a faculty exchange program between the Mandel School and EOTVOS Lorand University (ELTE) in Hungary, funded by the U.S. Information Agency. Faculty assisted ELTE with developing advanced social work degree programs, and ELTE faculty assisted the Mandel School with "internationalizing" its curriculum.

Faculty and students also visited and conducted research at the orphanage for the "irrecuperables" in Hirlau, Romania. International scholars and social workers visited MSASS and the Mandel Center throughout the 1990s, collaborating with faculty and students regarding the development of foster care systems, social services delivery, organizational practices, and curriculum creation. Johnson and fellow faculty member Victor Groza traveled to Romania to provide technical assistance and training to community organizations. In 1997-98, Groza assisted in a community HIV prevention project in Bucharest, Hungary. Faculty also developed collaborative relationships with social work professionals in Russia and Ghana.

In 1993, Ilga Svechs completed a Fulbright year in her native Latvia, where she taught courses, assisted in the creation of social work educational content, and conducted research at the local children's hospital. In 1994, Hokenstad visited both Canterbury University in Christchurch, New Zealand and the National Institute of Social Work in London, where he conducted a research project studying developmental models designed to help the elderly manage at home. This work continued throughout the late 1990s as Hokenstad and Baila Miller led an interdisciplinary team of University faculty in creating a training program in home and community-based care for the elderly. This program taught social workers from 15 countries throughout Eastern Europe and the former Soviet Union with funding from the Open Society Institute of New York City.

Under Dean Bailey, the Mandel School created the Local International Konnections (LINK) Committee, which sponsored activities related to international social work, including an international student reception, brown bag discussions, mentorships for workers in the Cleveland International Program, and the development of a course in International Travel and Study. The Committee also sponsored a Colloquium on Baltic States in 1995, which included social workers from Lithuania and Latvia. In 1997-98, LINK became a student-run caucus and part of the MSASS Student Coordinating Board, sponsoring the popular Multicultural Awareness Days, guest speakers, and celebrations for Hispanic Heritage Month. The LINK program helped cement the School's reputation as internationally-focused and helped attract international students.

In 1997-98, faculty created a new course concentration in international social work, and the School established the Herman D. Stein Lecture in International Social Work. The first Stein lecturer was Moshe Kerem, an eminent Israeli educator and leader of the kibbutz movement.

Students participated in a summer exchange course program sponsored by European Institute of Comparative Social Studies, attending classes in The Netherlands and England. The School also established collaborative agreements with the University of Bucharest in Hungary and Helwan University in Egypt. These programs were the building blocks of what became the School's strong commitment to international partnerships, global education, and study abroad programs.

+ Dean M.C. "Terry" Hokenstad with the International Awareness Days showcase in 1996.

+ Claudia Coulton teaching a class in November, 1995.

League of Greater Cleveland in 1992). Each student was given a mentoring team, career planning training, summer job placements, and test taking classes. The Cleveland Teacher Partnership with East, Glenville, and Lincoln-West High Schools also flourished, as faculty and staff partnered with teachers to develop and implement retention programs for freshmen. The program served over 600 students and forty teachers per year.

MSASS also maintained its commitment to examining state, local, and national policies on substance abuse and creating coursework to assist social workers in addressing addiction. In 1990, it was awarded a five-year, $347,000 Faculty Development Clinical Training Grant by the National Institute on Alcohol and Alcohol Abuse (NIAAA), the National Institute on Drug Abuse (NIDA), and the Office of Substance Abuse Prevention. With National Institute on Drug Abuse funding, MSASS and University researchers created "Project Newborn" in 1994, which is a longitudinal study of hundreds of mothers and their children exposed prenatally to alcohol and cocaine, tracing its effects over time and following the children from birth until their early 20s.

Local and State Collaboration

MSASS continued to reach out to the community. It partnered with Cleveland State University

School of Social Work, the Ohio Chapter of NASW, and local social workers to hold a teach-in day highlighting the plight of individuals in poverty on October 20, 1992. That same year, the School also created a joint program with Baldwin Wallace College's Division of Education to offer MSSA students the option of earning an Ohio School Social Worker Certification, making MSASS the sponsor of one of only two school social worker programs in the state.

The School also remained committed to providing training for family and children's services executives and staff throughout Ohio. The Center for Public Sector Leadership and Service (CPSLS), directed by John Yankey and Zoe Breen Wood, PhD 2012, worked to assist public sector agencies with education, training, research, and organizational development. The CPSLS created field work projects with the Cuyahoga County Department of Children and Family Services as well as with a public agency in Erie County, Pennsylvania. Be-

yond providing classes, the School assisted the Ohio Department of Human Services, Office of Child Care and Family Services in securing federal funding to allow employees of county agencies to earn master's degrees. By 1994, 20 students from Cuyahoga and Summit counties had enrolled in the School's Intensive Semester program. The School also used federal funding to assist Ohio in developing new curriculum for child welfare. Beyond this, CPSLS hosted an Institute for Civil Society Development in 1995-96 that worked to institutionalize community-building techniques to assist developing democracies, linking the School's local and international outreach.

By 1999, the transformations that had occurred both in Cleveland and on campus placed the MSASS on the cutting edge of addressing poverty, building community relationships, and forming international partnerships. The Mandel School of Applied Social Sciences was prepared to continue its work into not only a new century but a new millennium. +

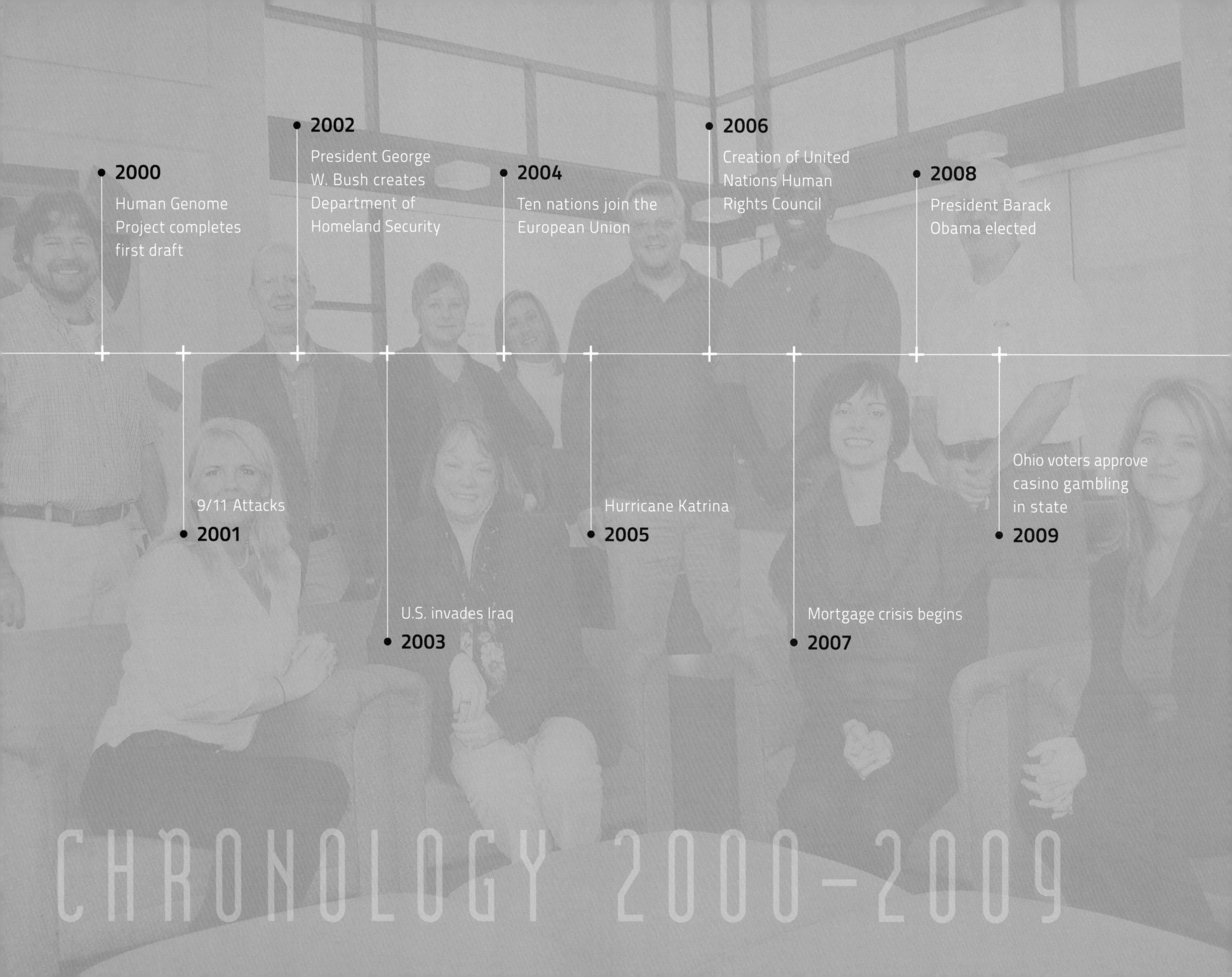

2000

Human Genome Project completes first draft

2002

President George W. Bush creates Department of Homeland Security

2004

Ten nations join the European Union

2006

Creation of United Nations Human Rights Council

2008

President Barack Obama elected

9/11 Attacks

2001

U.S. invades Iraq

2003

Hurricane Katrina

2005

Mortgage crisis begins

2007

Ohio voters approve casino gambling in state

2009

CHRONOLOGY 2000-2009

CHAPTER 9

A Center for Excellence

As the Mandel School of Applied Social Sciences entered the twenty-first century, it maintained a strong commitment to "community-based practice," which Dean Bailey described as "grounded in the belief that the community and the School are best served when they work in partnership." Despite the financial challenges that both Case Western Reserve and the city of Cleveland experienced during the 2000s, and the crisis that the United States faced in the aftermath of the 9/11 attacks, MSASS maintained and expanded its focus on community outreach, service, and the cause of social change and justice in the wider world.

Fighters Who Are Going to Change the World

MSASS was nationally prominent during the 2000s, ranked in the top 10 of schools of social work by *U.S. News & World Report* (and #1 in Ohio). With the generosity of major donors and friends, new programs, research centers, and endowed chairs helped the School further its mission. The Mandel Foundation continued its strong support, providing an "evergreen" yearly renewable grant of $850,000 designed to help the School focus on its "most important strategic priorities." In the doctoral program, the Mandel Leadership Fellows program continued admitting students. The Mandel Scholars Program also continued throughout the 2000s, with yearly luncheons held for students to present their research. The Mandel Scholars were chosen each year by a committee made up of faculty, admissions staff, and field advisors and given awards in two categories: the Dean Scholars, who received full tuition, and the Merit Scholars, who received up

+ Cover of the 2000 Mandel School Viewbook, "The Path of Heart."

+ Mandel Scholars luncheon in 2008 with Jack, Joseph and Morton Mandel and Dean Grover C. Gilmore *(Nannette Bedway)*.

to $12,000 per year. At the 2008 luncheon, Morton L. Mandel reminded the Scholars that they were "the fighters who are going to change the world." In 2007, MSASS and the Mandel Center for Nonprofit Organizations jointly awarded Jack, Joseph and Morton Mandel the first annual Advocate for Social Justice and Leadership Development Award.

Former Congressman and Distinguished Visiting Professor Louis Stokes and Arthur Naparstek created the Louis Stokes Scholarship in Community and Development and Management in 2001 with $1.3 million in federal funding. The scholarships were given annually to five African-American and Hispanic students entering the MSSA program to train as professionals in community development. Students in the program earned degrees at the School while working full-time, attending classes through the School's Intensive Weekend program.

+ Congressman Louis Stokes with Intensive Weekend MSSA students.

CONGRESSMAN LOUIS STOKES:
Civil Rights Champion, Distinguished Visiting Professor (1998–2015), and Friend

It's not often a civil rights icon can be a class speaker, but that was a regular occurrence for nearly 20 years when Congressman Louis Stokes was appointed a Distinguished Visiting Professor at the Mandel School after retiring from a 30-year career in government in 1998.

"He truly has made a difference in our nation, our region, and in the lives of our students and faculty. Each semester I read the wonderful teaching evaluations that he received. He brought advocacy and policy reform to life, and he was generous in giving his time and wisdom to everyone," said Dean Gilmore.

In the 1970s, Dean Hokenstad worked with Stokes to establish the Washington Semester program. Once on faculty, Stokes made a significant impact. He and Dean Naparstek

+ Congressman Louis Stokes on campus *(Dan Milner)*.

designed the Louis Stokes Fellowship Program, which focuses on educating African-American and Hispanic professionals in community development to transform urban neighborhoods and improve the quality of life for residents through economic, housing and civic development.

Students also benefitted from Stokes' guest lectures on social policy and civil rights. His message was powerful and clear: "There is nothing better than the opportunity to serve people. Continue to stand for and believe in justice, eliminate impediments to equal opportunity, use your education to help people and seek justice for those who don't have it."

Stokes often told social work students, "I want to thank you [social workers]. You sure changed my life." Stokes grew up poor in a low-income Cleveland neighborhood and was visited by social workers as a child—including Mandel School alumna, Ella Mae Cheeks Johnson, MSSA 1928 (profiled in Chapter 1), who made a lasting impression as someone who did her job with compassion.

Stokes died August 18, 2015, just a few months after celebrating his 90th birthday at the Mandel School. Shortly after, a new award was created in his honor: the Louis Stokes Community Leadership award recognizes alumni who embody "the socially-minded characteristics of the late beloved and honorable Congressman Louis Stokes and emulate his spirit in the community." The first recipient was Maria Thompson, MSSA 2005.

ALUMNI PROFILE:
India Pierce Lee, MSSA 2005

A former air traffic controller, India Pierce Lee is now directing essential funding to Greater Cleveland's most critical needs in her role as Senior Vice President, Program at the Cleveland Foundation, where she leads the foundation's grantmaking team.

Pierce Lee joined the foundation in 2006 as Program Director for Neighborhoods, Housing and Community Development. She worked with Cleveland's community development corporations and neighborhood intermediary organizations, and oversaw the Greater University Circle Initiative, a multi-institutional neighborhood revitalization partnership. Prior to joining the Cleveland Foundation, Pierce Lee served as Senior Vice President of Programs at Neighborhood Progress Inc.

She received a Louis Stokes Fellowship in Community Development from the Mandel School to pursue her MSSA. In 2009, Pierce Lee completed the prestigious Loeb Fellowship from the Graduate School of Design at Harvard University, where she studied neighborhood revitalization, with a special interest in sustainability. She completed a Master of Art in Psychology specializing in Diversity Management at Cleveland State University in 2017.

+ India Pierce Lee in 2015
(Maria Sharron).

+ Grace F. Brody (center) with Victor Groza
and Dean Grover C. Gilmore.

The first Stokes Fellows enrolled in 2002, and by 2007, the program had 21 graduates.

The generosity of several major donors led to the creation of new research centers and endowed chairs:

- With funding from Ruth W. Begun of the Society for the Prevention of Violence, MSASS established the interdisciplinary Dr. S.J. and Ruth Begun Center for Anti-Violence Research and Education and the Begun Professorship in 1999, which is currently held by Daniel Flannery.
- Rocco Motto donated to create the Verna Houck Motto Chair for Families and Communities, honoring his wife Verna, MSSA 1942. The new chair

was linked to the School's Cuyahoga County Early Childhood Initiative. It is currently held by Gerald Mahoney.

- Grace F. Brody endowed the Grace F. Brody Chair in Parent-Child Studies, to honor her longtime interest in helping social workers build relationships between parents and their children. It is currently held by Victor Groza.

Dean Bailey continued to serve until 2002, when she was succeeded by Grover "Cleve" Gilmore, then the Associate Dean of the College of Arts and Sciences and Professor of Psychology at Case Western Reserve. At the same time, several longtime faculty members retired during the 2000s, including Baila Miller; Marvin Rosenberg, PhD 1968, MSSA 1962; Ilga Svechs; Kathleen Wells; and Pranab Chatterjee. Mark Singer, PhD 1983, MSSA 1979, was appointed the new Leonard W. Mayo Professor in Family and Child Welfare.

In the master's degree program, faculty continued developing the Ability-Based Learning Environment (ABLE) and conducted a significant redesign of the direct practice concentration, introduced in 2008. In the foundation curriculum, two new courses were added. The first was a new course in direct

BEGUN CENTER FOR VIOLENCE PREVENTION RESEARCH AND EDUCATION:
Solutions for a Safer and Healthier Tomorrow

Established by anti-violence pioneer Ruth W. Begun in 1999, the center was originally called the Dr. S. J. and Ruth Begun Center for Anti-Violence Research and Education. It was dedicated toward preventing violent and asocial behavior and working to address the effects of violence upon society. Ruth Begun also provided funding for the creation of the Semi J. and Ruth W. Begun Professorship, with the Begun Professor serving as director of the Begun Center.

In 2011, the Institute for the Study and Prevention of Violence, which was founded in 1998 and housed at Kent State University, moved to the Mandel School and merged to form the Begun Center for Violence Prevention Research and Education. Today, Daniel Flannery is the Semi J. and Ruth W. Begun Professor and director of the Begun Center, leading a staff of experts in research, community outreach, training, technical assistance, and evaluation. They represent multiple disciplines, including social work, psychology, education, anthropology, criminal justice, and sociology.

The Begun Center partners with multiple organizations in the community, legal system, behavioral health sciences, and government to offer program evaluation services, research, training, and assistance in implementing evidence-based practices. Two major initiatives are the Center for Innovative Practices (CIP) and the Partnership for Evaluation, Research and Implementation (PERI). CIP assists community-based agencies in improving outcomes for children and their families and provides training in several evidence-based practices, including Multi-Systemic Therapy, Intensive Home-Based Treatment, Functional Family Therapy, and the Integrated Co-occurring Treatment Model. PERI, founded in 2015 and directed by Jeff Kretschmar, assists human services nonprofit organizations in evaluating their effectiveness, quality, and program implementation. Funded by the George Gund Foundation, St. Luke's Foundation, and the O'Neill Foundation, PERI assists nonprofits that might otherwise not be able to afford evaluation services.

In recent years, the Center has worked with the Cuyahoga County Prosecutor's Office on the Cuyahoga County Sexual Assault Kit Task Force, which tests and analyzes the County's backlog of untested rape kits. To date, the Task Force has lead to over 500 indictments and 200 convictions. Begun Center research has revealed new ways to investigate rape and sexual assault. The Begun Center has also assisted the city of Cleveland with the opioid epidemic, youth violence prevention program, and created a new method of assessing trauma in children, particularly those involved in the juvenile court system.

+ The staff of the Begun Center for Violence Prevention Research and Education in 2008.

The Eight Abilities and the Ability-Based Learning Environment (ABLE)

In the late 1990s, the School began to develop what it called the Eight Abilities, skills that the faculty deemed essential for a person to develop in order to competently practice social work at the master's degree level. Under the leadership of Wallace J. Gingerich, the School launched the first classes that incorporated the abilities in 1996-97. This evolved into the groundbreaking Ability-Based Learning Environment (ABLE), which was fully implemented in 2002 and has served as a innovative model for other social work schools.

ABLE is a competency-based model of social work education created to allow students to develop skills to "address the most complex human and community problems." The Eight Abilities are at the center of all learning opportunities, including coursework and field education:

- Identify as a Reflective Professional Social Worker
- Advocate for Social, Economic, and Environmental Justice
- Apply Social Work Practice Methods
- Uphold Social Work Values and Ethics
- Integrate Cultural, Economic, and Global Diversity
- Think Critically About Theory and Research Knowledge
- Communicate Effectively
- Develop as a Social Work Leader

practice methods and skills with individuals and families, in which students participated in a laboratory course where they videotaped themselves working with a "client." A second methods course on social work with groups, communities, and organizations was added to allow students to encounter the full range of social work experiences.

In the advanced curriculum, two required courses were added: Problem Identification, Screening and Assessment, and Theory and Practice Approaches.

+ Doctoral students in 2007.

The faculty also made updates to coursework in the direct practice specializations—aging, alcohol and other drug abuse, children, youth and families, health, or mental health—as well as the electives.

A revised doctoral curriculum was implemented in 2001 with new electives and a renewed focus on research. Coursework was redesigned to add additional micro theory content, to train students in interdisciplinary work, and to help meet the need for teachers with doctorates in the field of social work education. The new curriculum included revised qualitative and quantitative research courses and classes in leadership and theory and methods of teaching. The doctoral program began to publish a newsletter for students called CONNECT. Students in the program were awarded fellowships from the Center on Urban Poverty and Community Development, the Cuyahoga County Community Mental Health Research Institute, the Grace F. Brody Institute for Parent-Child Studies, the Gund Foundation, and the Dean's Office, among others. With donations from family and friends, the School also created the Arol Shack Dissertation Award to honor

Shack, a longtime doctoral program department assistant who died in 2007.

In 2008, the Nancy Lyon Porter Scholarship was established for a student in the community development concentration, honoring Porter's work with the Center for Community Solutions and the School's Visiting Committee. The Mandel School also created an agreement with Lourdes College in Toledo, Ohio, to allow students to complete part of their MSSA degree at Lourdes and the rest in the School's Intensive Weekend program. The School also established a relationship with National Chi Nan University in Taiwan for students to come to MSASS to complete doctorates.

Research Productivity and Outreach

A strong commitment to research endured. In 2008, the faculty were the second most productive in research at Case Western Reserve. In 1999, the School created a Research and Training

+ Sarah S. Andrews (second from right) with a group of students in 2005.

Interim Dean, 1992–1994
WALLACE J. GINGERICH, PHD
Set National Standards for Ability-Based Learning

A native of Iowa, Wallace J. Gingerich was inspired to pursue a career in social work by the Mennonite values of pacifism and service that he learned during his childhood. He earned a bachelor's degree in sociology from Goshen College in 1966 and an MSW (1968) and PhD (1975) from Washington University in St. Louis. Before pursuing his doctorate, he worked as a psychiatric social worker in California.

In 1990, Gingerich joined MSASS as a professor, then served as Interim Dean, twice as the Associate Dean for Academic Affairs, and as the founding Director of the Office of Educational Assessment. Gingerich was instrumental in developing the Ability-Based Learning Environment (ABLE), which emphasized abilities that students needed to develop to become effective social workers. The innovative program set national standards for social work education.

Throughout his career, Gingerich wrote multiple articles on solution-focused brief therapy, ability-based learning, practice evaluation, and the use of computer technology in social work. Upon his retirement in 2010, Gingerich became a Professor Emeritus, continued to teach, and served as the first conciliation counselor for the University's newly-formed Faculty Conciliation and Mediation Program. He fully retired in 2014.

+ Interim Dean Wallace Gingerich in 1990.

Advisory Committee. Victor Groza was appointed Associate Dean of Research and Training. To reward and encourage innovation in research, a Mandel Research Development Fund was established to support faculty and staff initiatives. Federal funding for research also continued, including a National Institute of Drug Abuse (NIDA) research infrastructure building grant given in 1999–2000 that supported the work of six faculty members.

The School's national prominence in the field of social work continued during the 2000s. Louis Stokes was appointed to the federal Commission on 21st Century Education in Science, Technology, Engineering, and Mathematics in 2006. Two years later, Robert Fischer authored a paper for the White House Conference on Research Related to the Faith-Based and Community Initiative. In 2009, both Claudia Coulton, PhD 1978, and Mark Joseph testified before U.S. House of Representatives subcommittees, Coulton on the foreclosure crisis and Joseph on public housing. Representing the School's impact on the field of social work, the 20th edition of the *Encyclopedia of Social Work* was published, containing entries from nine MSASS faculty and 13 former faculty and alumni.

Community engagement and outreach to Cleveland and Northeast Ohio was also strengthened. In 2008, the community development concentration faculty began a partnership with the Northeast Ohio Alliance for Hope (NOAH) to work toward increased civic engagement in East Cleveland. With funding from the Case Western Reserve Office of Community Partnerships, students surveyed East Cleveland residents and the School organized parent patrols at the city's five elementary schools. This partnership between the University and community partners culminated in the East Cleveland Partnership, housed at the Center on Urban Poverty and Community Development.

The research centers and institutes also were instrumental in the task of community building and outreach. The Begun Center, Cuyahoga County Community Mental Health Initiative, and the Poverty Center continued their work in anti-violence, mental health research, and anti-poverty advocacy. A team led by Coulton provided technical assistance to the Cuyahoga County Department of Children and Family Services to improve

+ The staff of the Center for Urban Poverty and Community Development, 2009.

services for children in foster care. In 2000, the Joseph and Florence Mandel Alzheimer's Caregiving Institute completed a five-year study of social support among family caregivers funded by the National Institute on Aging. The Center for Public Sector Leadership and Service assisted public service agencies and school districts in programs benefitting child welfare. In 2000, the Center also served as a home for MSASS programs assisting "civil society development" in Romania. The

+ David Crampton teaching.

CENTER FOR EVIDENCE-BASED PRACTICES

The Center for Evidence-Based Practices (CEBP) began as the Ohio Substance Abuse and Mental Illness Coordinating Center of Excellence (SAMI CCOE) in December 1999, an offshoot of the Mandel School's Cuyahoga County Community Mental Health Research Institute. A collaboration with the Department of Psychiatry at Case Western Reserve, it was founded under the leadership of Lenore Kola and David Biegel from the Mandel School, Robert J. Ronis of the Department of Psychiatry, and Director of Clinical Training Patrick E. Boyle, MSSA 1999, PhD 2016.

CEBP received funding from the Ohio Department of Mental Health to serve 13 community organizations to provide assistance in implementing the New Hampshire-Dartmouth Dual Disorder Integrated Treatment model (now the Integrated Dual Disorder Treatment, or IDDT).

In 2005, CEBP created the Ohio Supported Employment Coordinating Center of Excellence (SE CCOE). In 2007, the SAMI CCOE created the "Tobacco and Recovery" service model for tobacco cessation with funding from the Ohio Tobacco Prevention Foundation. The model was renamed and expanded into "Tobacco: Recovery Across the Continuum" (TRAC) in 2009. Other programs that the Center provided implementation assistance for during the 2000s included Motivational Interviewing (MI) and Benefits Planning (BP).

In 2013, CEBP created a third CCOE: the Assertive Community Treatment Coordinating Center of Excellence, or ACT CCOE, to help train organizations to assist individuals with severe mental illness in avoiding homelessness, hospitalization, or encounters with the criminal justice system.

In recent years, CEBP has continued its mission by providing training for probation officers and employees of housing services agencies, partnering with the Veterans Affairs Administration to implement IDDT, and establishing a Job Board. It has also taken steps to address Ohio's growing heroin and opioid addiction crisis by working closely with the Ohio Department of Mental Health and Addiction Services. In 2009, the Mandel School was given the Bronze Key Award from Recovery Resources, the regional affiliate of the National Council for Alcohol and Drug Dependence in Cleveland, for innovations in the field of dual diagnosis, in particular the creation of the SAMI CCOE.

Mandel School completed evaluation reports for the Early Childhood Initiative Evaluation for Cuyahoga County from 2000-2003 and became the home of a "Research Annex" providing offices for a national team of researchers from the University of North Carolina and University of Chicago.

In 2004, the Mandel School created a new research center: The Center on Interventions for Children and Families (CICF), founded by Mahoney and Groza with funding from the U.S. Department of Education. Its mission was to educate parents on child care strategies and to provide information on childhood development. In 2005, it created the CICF Early Intervention Clinic, and two years later created a new curriculum called Responsive Teaching. By 2008, the CICF worked with 37 trainees from

CHILD WELFARE FELLOWS PROGRAM:
Developing a Highly-Trained Workforce

Created in 2009, the Child Welfare Fellows program assists child welfare agencies across Northeast Ohio with developing highly-trained staff. Funded by the National Child Welfare Workforce Institute (NCWWI), the program seeks to remove barriers preventing employees of child welfare agencies from pursuing master's degrees by offering scholarships to individuals who serve as full-time staff for public child welfare agencies in Cuyahoga, Summit, Lorain, Lake, Medina, Stark, Ashtabula, Geauga, Richfield, Huron, or Trumbull counties.

To qualify for the program, which is directed by Victor Groza, applicants needed to have already earned a bachelor's degree, demonstrate an existing two- to three-year commitment to their agency, and meet the qualifications for the Intensive Weekend MSSA program. Students enter each year as a cohort and complete field placements within their employing agencies, but in a different department from where they normally work.

Since 2009, NCWWI has provided $1.3 million in funding support, including a four-year, $588,000 grant in 2015 that allowed expansion to additional counties. The Mandel School, which is one of only 13 schools funded nationally, offsets the remaining tuition costs not covered by the grant.

MSASS, speech and hearing sciences, and nursing, and had reached over 150 families. The Responsive Teaching curriculum was adopted by one-third of county early intervention programs run by the Ohio Department of Mental Retardation and Developmental Disabilities.

MSASS International

In the aftermath of the 9/11 attacks, MSASS remained committed to international outreach and openness—and even increasing it throughout the decade. The School's Office of International Affairs for Social Welfare and Non-Governmental Organizations, directed by Soad Mansour, MSSA 1972,

+ Visiting students from Korea.

supported international students, facilitated study abroad trips, and hosted visitors. The Office expanded the School's International Advisory Committee, helped students earn an interdisciplinary certificate in global health, developed international field placements, and worked with the Local INternational Konnections (LINK) group. In 2004–2005, the Office helped the Mandel School develop a popular travel study program, and by decade's end, had sent faculty, students, staff, and alumni on trips to Guatemala, Kenya, Tanzania, Israel, El Salvador, India, Bangladesh, Ecuador, Ukraine, the Dominican Republic, the Netherlands, and Greece. In 2008, Dean Gilmore referred to this outreach as "MSASS International."

The School's faculty was also highly active internationally. In 2000, Terry Hokenstad served as a co-chair for the U.S. Committee for the Celebration of the United Nations' International Year of the Older Person, and served with the International Association of Schools of Social Work, an NGO that worked with the United Nations to address aging issues internationally. Groza continued to consult with orphanages in Romania and the Ukraine on establishing foster care systems and in 2006 began to work with UNICEF on improving child welfare in Guatemala. The Mandel School hosted international visitors throughout the decade, including a group from the Korean Social Work Association in 2007. That same year, the Council on Social Work Education named MSASS as one of their "Partners in Advancing Education for International Social Work," honoring the School's commitment to international advocacy, outreach, and social justice.

The School's Alumni Association continued its successful fundraising throughout the decade, raising over $100,000 yearly for the Annual Fund, which supported student scholarships. The Alumni continued the popular "match" program that paired alumni with first year students, as well as the one-to-one mentoring program that matched doctoral students with faculty members. They held a professional education conference yearly and sponsored social events to bring

+ Students in the lounge area, 2005.

faculty, students, staff, and alumni together. One popular event was the "Dollars for Scholars Garage Sale," which sold donated goods to the University community. The proceeds went to support the Annual Fund.

In a 2008 speech, Case Western Reserve University President Barbara R. Snyder noted the service and outreach that MSASS students gave to the community—through their field placements, students provided over 224,000 hours of service per year! Beyond the classroom, the student-led caucuses at the School conducted multiple community and university-based projects. MSASS students were well represented nationally, winning three of the six doctoral dissertation prizes given at the National Symposium on Doctoral Research in Social Work in 2002. Students also won awards and scholarships from the State of Ohio, participated in international relief efforts, and presented at major national conferences.

The School embraced the technological possibilities of the new century, creating its first Office of Information Technology, which was later renamed in honor of Roberto Flores, its first director, who died suddenly in 2000. The School's Harris Library incorporated new technology into its facility and collections, updating its computers, adding electronic journals to its collection, redesigning its website, and allowing patrons to email research

requests. In 2006, the library hired a new director, Samantha Skutnik, and sponsored a program to donate dictionaries to students at Forest Hills Elementary School in East Cleveland. Two years later, the library honored the 100th birthday of its namesake, Lillian F. Harris, MSSA 1933, with a celebratory tea party. Harris later donated $20,000 to establish an endowment to support library operations, particularly technology purchases.

As the Mandel School of Applied Social Sciences completed the first decade of a new century, it remained more dedicated than ever to community-based practice, reflecting its long history of engagement with Cleveland, Northeast Ohio, the nation, and the world. By honoring that history, the Mandel School family prepared to not only celebrate its past at an upcoming Centennial, but continue the hard work of being agents of change in the wider world. +

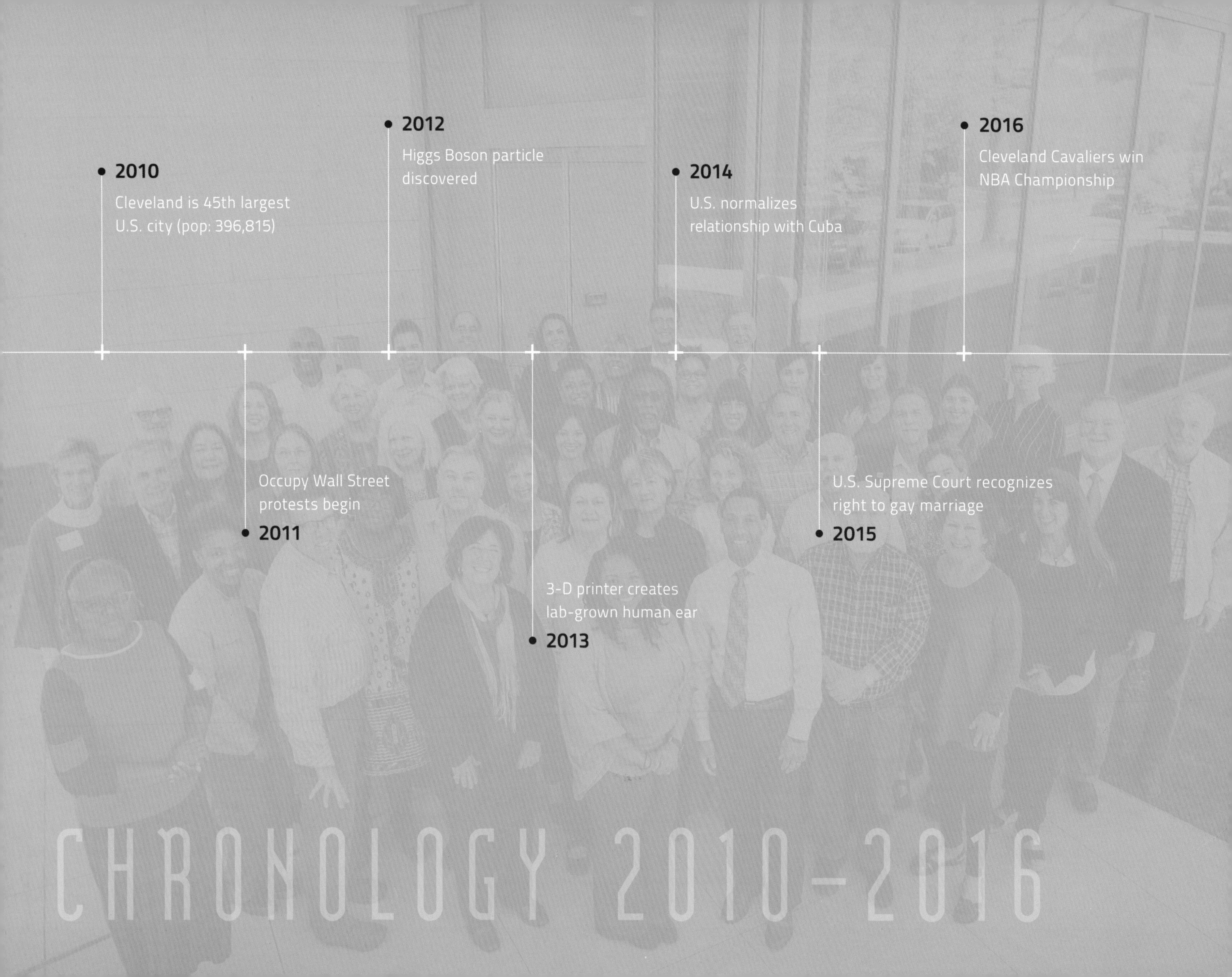

2010

Cleveland is 45th largest
U.S. city (pop: 396,815)

2012

Higgs Boson particle
discovered

2014

U.S. normalizes
relationship with Cuba

2016

Cleveland Cavaliers win
NBA Championship

Occupy Wall Street
protests begin

2011

U.S. Supreme Court recognizes
right to gay marriage

2015

3-D printer creates
lab-grown human ear

2013

CHRONOLOGY 2010-2016

CHAPTER 10

Change Agents Creating a More Just World

+ Doctoral student June-Yung Kim in 2016 *(Maria Sharron).*

During a two-year Centennial celebration beginning in 2015, which honored both the founding of the School in 1915 and its first classes in 1916, the School motto became "Inspiring Hope, Shaping the Future." Throughout the mid-2010s, the School reached out to the local community and the wider world—expanding its global study programs, enrolling more students in innovative ways, and increasing the work of its research centers and institutes.

Even as the city of Cleveland continued to struggle with the results of the foreclosure crisis, poverty, violence, and the emergence of the opioid crisis, the Mandel School remained committed to the task of meeting these problems and changing the world. By mid-decade, the School's outside funding for research had increased by nearly 270% from 2005,

Mandel School
1916
100
2016
Case Western Reserve University

INSPIRING HOPE. SHAPING THE FUTURE:
Centennial Celebration of 100 Years of Educational Excellence

The 100-year anniversary spanned 100 weeks during the 2015–2016 and 2016–2017 academic years to commemorate the School's founding in 1915 and its first class of students in 1916. The two-year celebration was planned and executed by a Centennial Planning Committee comprised of alumni, faculty, students, and staff that achieved:

- 2016 Reunion, with an awards luncheon that celebrated 100 alumni award-winners, a Dean's panel that reunited the current and former leaders of the School, and a free community block party that attracted more than 1,000 people
- Historical books on the history of the school's impact, made possible with the support of the Jack, Joseph and Morton Mandel Foundation
- More than $100,000 raised for the Centennial Endowed Scholarship Fund
- Establishment of the Mandel School Hall of Achievement
- Centennial Speaker Series—18 educational events and lectures

- Centennial Salons—12 gatherings held in Denver, Los Angeles, Atlanta, and Cleveland
- Service initiatives that benefited local charities and fostered student activism

Centennial Planning Committee
- Dean Grover C. Gilmore

Co-Chairs
- Kathleen J. Farkas, PhD 1984
- Denise Gibson, MSSA 1978
- John Yankey

Members
- Goldie Alvis, MSSA 1973
- Abigail Assmus, MSSA/MA 2017
- Paula Atwood, MSSA 1973
- Tracey Bradnan
- David Crampton
- Jazmine Danner, MSSA 2017

- Eric Dicken, MNO 2009
- Nada DiFranco, MNO 2008
- Beth Embrescia, MSSA 1994
- Robert L. Fischer
- Nora Hennessy, MNO 2004
- Nina Holzer, MSSA/MNO
- Annette Iwamoto, MSSA 2012
- Lenore A. Kola
- Marianne Lax, MSSA 1990
- Pat Nobili, MSSA 1983
- Melody Stewart, MSSA
- Elizabeth M. Tracy
- JoAnn White, MNO 1999

Sub-Committee Members: Sarah Andrews; Ina Brand; Mark Chupp; Kathi Gant, MSSA 1990; Beth Glas, MNO 2011; Adrienne Hatten, MNO 1996; Kristen Kirchgesler; Chris Hall, MSSA 1978, CNM 2001; June Hund; Samantha Skutnik; Amarinder Syan, MSSA 2017; Jennine Vlach, MNO 2016

+ Centennial Co-Chairs Kathleen Farkas, PhD 1984; John Yankey; and Denise Gibson, MSSA 1978 *(Maria Sharron).*

+ Mark Chapin, PhD 1995, and Lisa M. Pape, MSSA 1990, join Elizabeth Tracy prior to a Centennial Speaker Series event on "Serving Veterans."

+ Top left: Vivian Jackson, PhD 2008, former Dean Darlyne Bailey, and Sharon Milligan celebrating the Centennial Block Party *(Rob Muller)*. **Top right:** Students Jessica Switzer, Leah Adams, and Jenn Angelo celebrating with Breeanna Usher, MSSA 2016, at the Centennial Block Party on October 15, 2016 *(Rob Muller)*. **Bottom left:** Inspiring Hope, Shaping the Future: The Deans' Perspectives was an event on October 14, 2016, that gathered the current and former Deans to discuss the history of Mandel School leadership and impact *(Steve Zorc)*. **Bottom right:** Dorothy Faller, MSSA 1978, and Sonia Minnes, PhD 1998 *(Rob Muller)*.

exceeding $9.4 million in 2015–2016. The Mandel School maintained its *U.S. News & World Report* ranking in the top 10 social work master's degree programs, and enrollment at MSASS increased significantly, reaching a record 652 in 2016.

The Mandel School continued to innovate during the 2010s. MSASS entered the era of social media with the creation of a Facebook page in 2008, a Twitter feed (@MandelSchool) in 2010, a YouTube channel in 2014, and an Instagram account in 2015.

In 2012, the Mandel Center for Nonprofit Organizations' Master's of Nonprofit Organizations (MNO) program was moved to the Mandel School and its building was renamed the Jack, Joseph and Morton Mandel Community Studies Center, now home to the Poverty Center and Begun Center research staffs. The MNO program was active, hosting a well-received speaker series with support from the Gail and Elliott Schlang Philanthropic Fund, a donor-advised fund of the Jewish Feder-

ation of Cleveland, which brought local nonprofit leaders to campus to discuss changes in the philanthropic sector over the last century and their relevance to social change.

Dean Gilmore wrote in 2015 that "the School has constantly collaborated with our community partners to create effective education models so graduates can address the most complex human and community problems." Coursework at the Mandel School remained centered around the Ability-Based

+ **Left:** Jack, Joseph and Morton Mandel Community Studies Center *(Tim Safranek).* **Right:** Students at Case for Community Day in 2016 *(Maria Sharron).*

Jack, Joseph and Morton Mandel Dean in Applied Social Sciences, 2002–Present
GROVER "CLEVE" GILMORE, PhD
Leadership for the New Millennium

During his tenure as the second-longest serving dean in School history, Grover "Cleve" Gilmore has overseen several record-setting milestones:

- Dramatic increase in research funding, by more than fifty percent, to $9.4 million in 2015-16;
- Record-high enrollment, with 653 students in all program formats as of 2016-2017;
- Creation of the Online MSSA, Case Western Reserve's first online degree program, and the School's first undergraduate minor in social work;
- Completion of a $9.4 million renovation of the main school building and a two-year celebration of the School's Centennial.

And he's still in the classroom: Gilmore teaches a popular short-term study abroad course to the Netherlands each spring, where students explore social justice policies and practices in Dutch culture.

A Boston native, Gilmore earned his bachelor's degree in psychology from Brandeis University, and he pursued his master's and doctoral degrees from Johns Hopkins University in 1974. He joined the faculty of the psychology department at Case Western Reserve in 1975. As an Associate Professor, he received John S. Diekhoff Award for Distinguished Graduate Teaching and Mentoring. Before becoming Dean of the Mandel School in 2002, Gilmore served as chair of the psychology department, acting chair of the statistics department, and Associate Dean of the College of Arts and Sciences.

In 2013, a gift from the Jack, Joseph and Morton Mandel Foundation established an endowed deanship, at the time one of only two endowed deanships among the top ten U.S. schools of social work.

"It was with great pleasure that we celebrated the appointment of Cleve Gilmore as the Jack, Joseph and Morton Mandel Dean in Applied Social Sciences. Cleve's great influence is due to the values, talents and skills that he possesses," said Morton L. Mandel, Chairman and CEO of the Jack, Joseph and Morton Mandel Foundation.

Gilmore has received funding from the National Institutes of Health to support his research for over 35 years. With interdisciplinary teams, he has focused on identifying sensory and cognitive problems that affect a person's ability to perform at full potential and has pioneered methods to assist Alzheimer's disease patients to improve their perceptual and cognitive performance. Gilmore serves on several national and local boards, including the Cleveland Hearing and Speech Center, the University of New England, and the Graduate School of Social Work at the University of Denver.

+ **Right:** Morton L. Mandel and Dean Grover C. Gilmore at the Dean's Chair Ceremony *(Dan Milner)*.

EXTREME MAKEOVER:
Major Mandel Foundation Gift Launches Building Renovation, Name Change, and Keeps School at Forefront of Education and Research

In 2013, the Jack, Joseph and Morton Mandel Foundation gave the Mandel School an $8 million gift to fund several major endeavors:

- Renaming it the Jack, Joseph and Morton Mandel School of Applied Social Sciences, honoring the significant role that the Mandel brothers had in the School's success for more than 50 years.
- Part of the financial gift, $3.05 million, created an endowed deanship to provide the Jack, Joseph and Morton Mandel Dean in Applied Social Sciences with resources to quickly and innovatively meet challenges, seize opportunities and fulfill the mission of the Mandel School to promote social justice and empower communities through social work and nonprofit practice.
- The majority of the donation, $4.95 million, was a lead gift for a new capital campaign to fund a major renovation and expansion of the main school building. By 2015, the building was a quarter-century old, and the planned renovation was designed to provide faculty, staff, and students with collaborative meeting spaces, active classrooms, space for the School's research centers and institutes, and room for community gatherings.

Additonal major funding for the renovation was provided by The Higley Fund of the Cleveland Foundation, which gave $1 million to create research, collaboration, and education spaces in the building. The gift created The Albert and Beverly Higley Research Commons in the building on the second and third floors, honoring the family's long history with the School, which dated back to Mildred Higley's graduation in 1922.

Other major funding was a $750,000 gift from Holley Fowler Martens, MSSA 2007, and her husband Rob Martens, which created a new office suite named in honor of Zoe Breen Wood, PhD 2012, for the field placement, student services and academic affairs departments, as well as an active-learning classroom named for John Lisy, MSSA 1977. The Martens' gift also included a $150,000 matching gift challenge, which helped the School complete its $9.4 million building capital campaign by October 2015.

Funding for the new lobby, front entrance, and atrium was provided by a $500,000 donation from the Donald and Alice Noble Foundation and the area was named the Noble Commons. David Noble and his wife Gayle Noble, MSSA 1988, gave to honor the legacy of David's father Donald, a graduate of Western Reserve University. The renovation of the Harris Library was funded with a $500,000 gift from Seth and Lilli Harris to honor Lillian F. Harris, MSSA 1933, and her husband Milford J. Harris, the library's namesakes. Other significant support was given by Case Western Reserve board chairman Chuck Fowler and his wife Char Fowler, the Saint Luke's Foundation, the Cleveland Foundation, the John and Margie Wheeler Family Fund of the Cleveland Foundation, and the Gund Foundation.

In late 2013, the architectural firm Westlake Reed Leskosky was chosen to design the renovation and expanded space in the building; they later received an American Institute of Architects Merit Award for their work on the project. The new design, which met LEED's (Leadership in Energy and Environmental Design) Silver Certification Target, removed the cantilevered overhands on the second and third floors, added a glass curtain wall frame for the courtyard, renovated classrooms and office suites, and relocated the Harris Library to the first floor. The Higley Research Commons was added to the second and third floors, and multiple meeting spaces and "huddle rooms" were added throughout the building.

A "wallbreaking" ceremony was held to commemorate the beginning of construction on June 29, 2015, as well as the official kick-off of the two-year centennial celebration. Morton L. Mandel, University President Barbara R. Snyder, and Dean Gilmore used hammers to break through a "brick wall" created for the occasion. They reunited at the official building rededication ceremony on September 16, 2016, upon the conclusion of the successful renovation.

+ Morton L. Mandel, Barbara R. Snyder, and Dean Gilmore at the "wallbreaking" ceremony that kicked off the building's renovation and the centennial *(Tony Gray)*.

+ Inset: Renovation in progress *(School Archives)*. **Below:** Building dedication ribbon cutting on September 16, 2016. From left to right: Lilli Harris; Leah Adams, MSSA/MNO student; Seth Harris; Holley Martens, MSSA 2007; Case Western Reserve President Barbara R. Snyder; Gayle Noble, MSSA 1988; Morton L. Mandel; David Noble; James C. Wyant; Chuck Fowler; Dean Gilmore; Bruce Higley; Char Fowler; Sharon Higley Watts; Bob Eckardt; Margie Wheeler, MSSA 1970; Marcia Levine, MSSA 1966; Jazmine Danner, MSSA student; Christine Manning, MSSA 1997; and Ron Reed.

Learning Environment (ABLE), a competency-based model of social work education incorporating the Eight Abilities that the faculty identified as necessary to practice social work competently in the field.

After launching the Online MSSA in 2012, the Mandel School introduced a social work minor in 2013 and received accreditation from a new licensing authority, the Ohio Chemical Dependency Professionals Board (OCDPB), which oversaw certification and licensing for chemical-dependency counselors.

The Mandel School played an active role in a special commission formed in 2013 by the Association for Community Organization and Social Administration (ACOSA), which examined ways to advance macro practice in social work. In 2013, the community practice concentration expanded to become a two-year, 60-credit hour concentration called Community Practice for Social Change. Enrollment in the new concentration increased rapidly.

Faculty and staff stayed current with the latest trends in education, experimenting with active learning and "flipped classroom" techniques. In 2015-2016, Megan R. Holmes, Elizabeth M. Tracy, and Lori Longs Painter, MSSA 1987, incorporated these techniques into their classes that taught practical clinical practice skills. The flipped classroom reverses traditional classwork, with class time focused on peer-to-peer discussions, collab-

+ Megan R. Holmes in 2012 *(Steve Zorc)*.

oration on group projects and exercises, and video conferences with social work practitioners. When the building was renovated, four of the classrooms were designed to be active learning—the highest number of any academic building on campus.

The Mandel School exhibited national leadership in 2010, when it became the home for three years to the newly established American Academy of Social Work and Social Welfare (AASWSW),

a new professional organization for social workers that promoted research, celebrated excellence, and served as an information resource. Claudia J. Coulton, PhD 1978, was one of the organization's inaugural fellows, and Dean Gilmore helped craft the organization's mission statement. David Biegel was inducted into the Academy in 2013, followed by the induction of Mark Singer, PhD 1983, MSSA 1979, in 2014.

The School was highly visible at national conferences, with multiple faculty, students, and alumni presenting their research at meetings for the Society for Social Work and Research (SSWR), with Biegel and Tracy awarded as SSWR fellows in 2016. That same year, emerita faculty member Ilga Svechs was made an Honorary APsaA Member by the American Psychoanalytic Association, one of the few, if not only, social workers to receive this honor.

The Mandel School co-sponsored the 2015 Cuyahoga County Conference on Social Welfare, at Cleveland State University, and hosted the 2016 conference on campus. National recognition also came in 2015 from Catholic Charities USA, which presented medals to John Yankey and Zoe Breen Wood, PhD 2012, in honor of their work providing leadership development.

The School responded to conditions in Cleveland and Northeast Ohio, reaching out to the community as it dealt with the housing crisis, poverty, violence, and addiction—via research, field placements, and even faculty service. David Miller served on City Council for South Euclid, and became Council President in 2010. Biegel was appointed to the Alcohol, Drug Addiction and Mental Health Services Board of Cuyahoga County (ADAMHS) in 2010. Field advisor Kirsten Gail, MSSA 1991, was elected mayor of South Euclid, Ohio.

NATIONAL INITIATIVE ON MIXED-INCOME COMMUNITIES ADDRESSES SEGREGATION OF POVERTY

The National Initiative on Mixed-Income Communities (NIMC) was created in 2013 at the Mandel School by founding director Mark L. Joseph to serve as the go-to national resource on the study of mixed-income housing and to promote successful developments aimed at reducing urban poverty. It is housed within the Center on Urban Poverty and Community Development.

Beginning in the late 1990s, cities began to build mixed-income developments on the site of former public housing projects, planning to provide multiple rental and ownership options to residents with diverse income levels. Beginning in 2005, Joseph led a team of researchers at Case Western Reserve and the University of Chicago to study—with funding from the John D. and Catherine T. MacArthur Foundation, the Rockefeller Foundation, the Annie E. Casey Foundation, and the U.S. Department of Housing and Urban Development—four mixed-income developments. It was this research that sparked the formation of NIMC.

Today, NIMC provides a mixed-income database, research library, consultation, project evaluation, and technical assistance. Its clients include the Washington, D.C. Office of the Deputy Mayor for Planning and Economic Development, Cleveland Neighborhood Progress, the Cuyahoga County Metropolitan Housing Authority, the Jack, Joseph and Morton Mandel Foundation, the Cleveland Foundation, the George Gund Foundation, Lipton Group, and Trek Development Group. A key NIMC partner is the Center for the Study of Social Policy and Urban Strategies, Inc., with whom NIMC maintains the Mixed-Income Strategic Alliance, a "learning network" for housing developments.

+ Mark Joseph in 2012 (Steve Zorc).

The Poverty Center's NEO CANDO database continued to function as an essential resource for local media and government as they evaluated the results of industrial pollution and the foreclosure crisis on Cleveland neighborhoods. David Crampton chaired a reform panel examining the child welfare practices of the Cuyahoga County Department of Children and Family Services beginning in 2010. In 2014, Crampton and Coulton, along with faculty from the Schubert Center for Child Studies and the Center for Clinical Investigation at the School of Medicine, were awarded a $2.3 million grant from the Eunice Kennedy Shriver National Institute of Child Health and Human Development to investigate how neighborhood conditions influenced rates of child neglect.

The opiate and heroin epidemic hit Ohio and the city of Cleveland particularly hard, and the Mandel School was on the front lines in response. The Begun Center for Violence Prevention Research and Education evaluated local drug courts and medication-assisted treatment options. A research team led by Tracy studied the difficulties that female addicts in recovery experienced in reestablshing social networks in a study funded by the National Institutes of Health's National Institute on Drug Abuse (NIDA). Project Newborn, a longitudinal study examining the long term effects of prenatal drug and alcohol exposure on children led by Sonia Minnes,

PhD 1998, received a four-year, $2.5 million federal grant to continue the study as the subjects moved into their early twenties.

The East Cleveland Partnership received new funding from alumni donors and Third Federal Savings and Loan. Partnering with local residents, nonprofits, churches, and businesses, the Mandel School held retreats for the East Cleveland's mayor and city council, worked with local leaders to

assess youth development needs, and surveyed vacant properties to help the city secure federal funding. Other local outreach included partnering with the Cleveland Foundation's Neighborhood Connections community-building program in 2015 to host Neighbor Up Network Night, facilitated by students, faculty, and alumni.

Unrest in Cleveland between police and the African-American community was also addressed.

+ Students protest the killing of Trayvon Martin in 2012.

The Begun Center worked with local law enforcement to promote nonviolence by developing Fugitive Safe Surrender programs, training local police to make referrals to mental health agencies, and assisting police with implementing the federal Byrne Criminal Justice Initiative. In late 2014, responding to the death of 12-year-old Tamir Rice after a confrontation with police, then-student Shelly Gracon, MSSA 2016, worked with Rice's family and teachers to create the Butterfly Project with funding from Cleveland City Councilman Matt Zone. The Project's first initiative was a summer camp for children aged 5-15, and Gracon then worked with camp participants to build a butterfly-shaped garden at Cudell Recreation Center. Mark Chupp and students participated by facilitating a day of contemplation and action on the one-year anniversary of Rice's death, with training to be facilitators at Butterfly Project-sponsored community dialogues.

The Mandel School's international outreach greatly expanded during the 2010s, with faculty conducting training for government officials and NGO leaders in Ethiopia in 2010, hosting PBS travel show host Rick Steves at the 2014 Reunion, and participating in an exchange program with criminology students from The Netherlands and with faculty from West University in Timisoara, Romania. Terry Hokenstad, who spent much of his career

INTERNATIONAL CHANGE AGENTS:
Global Education and Study Abroad

During the 2010s, the Mandel School embarked on a significant expansion of its global education, building upon a longstanding tradition of faculty and students travelling overseas and the establishment of a full-fledged study abroad program of 3-credit courses during the 2000s.

By 2016, the program offered seven courses in five nations—offering one-third of all of the University's short-term study abroad options. Held during the University's winter and spring breaks, the courses are available to not only Case Western Reserve students, but also students from other universities, exposing them to new cultures and providing hands-on experience in social work in other countries and settings.

Throughout the decade, courses were offered in The Netherlands, Bangladesh, India, Russia, Poland, Turkey, Guatemala, Ecuador, Ghana, and Sub-Saharan Africa. The Director of International Programs from 2007-15 was Deborah Jacobson, who was succeeded by Mark Chupp, PhD 2003. In 2016, the School created the Ronald A. Stewart Fund for International Study and Service, which provided students with scholarships to engage in study and service around the globe. Ronald A. Stewart, MNO 1996, was a participant in four of the School's study abroad programs.

Case Western Reserve was named one of the 25 best colleges and universities for LGBT students, in large part due to the Mandel School's study abroad course examining the LGBT experience in The Netherlands.

+ **Top:** Ecuador Study Abroad Course, 2015.
Bottom: Netherlands Study Abroad course, 2015.

100 CENTENNIAL ALUMNI AWARD WINNERS

These extraordinary alumni were recognized at 2016 Homecoming+Reunion for professional success, achievement and leadership in social work and nonprofit management throughout the Mandel School's history. They were also inducted into the newly-established Mandel School Hall of Achievement, in recognition of their impact and importance in their respective fields and to the school.

Distinguished Alumni Award

Alumni who demonstrate extraordinary professional success and achievement over the span of their entire careers of 25 or more years.

Georgia Anetzberger, MSSA 1980, PhD 1986
Lowell Arye, MSSA 1982
Paula Atwood, MSSA 1973
Hoda Badran, DSW 1967
Myrna Balk, MSSA 1963
James Billups, MSSA 1954
Margaret Brodkin, MSSA 1967
Dorothy Burnside, MSSA 1947
Allen Cohen, MSSA 1959
Susan Cole, PhD 2001
Anita Curry-Jackson, MSSA 1970
Hope Curfman, MSSA 1942
Maureen Dee, MSSA 1978
Charles Emlet, PhD 1998
Dorothy Faller, MSSA 1975

Gerald Futty, MSSA 1958
Denise Gibson, MSSA 1978
Stuart Gitlin, MSSA 1973
Jean Greenhaigh, MSSA 1946
Eliezer Jaffe, MSSA 1957, DSW 1960
Robert Keefe, MSSA 1985
Jean Lawrence, MSSA 1984
Art Lifson, MSSA 1969
Wayne Lindstrom, PhD 1986
Soad Mansour, MSSA 1972
Lillian Milanof, MSSA 1949
Patricia "Pat" Nobili, MSSA 1983
Lisa Pape, MSSA 1990
David Pedlar, PhD 1997
Ted Rubin, MSSA 1950
Nancy Schiffer, MSSA 1971
Harvey Shankman, MSSA 1974
Seymour Slavin, MSSA 1958
Norman Sohn, MSSA 1968
Melody Stewart, PhD 2008
Ella Thomas, MSSA 1971
Eleanor Weisberger Weintraub, MSSA 1943
Margaret "Margie" Wheeler, MSSA 1970
Gautam Yadama, MSSA 1985, PhD 1990

Professional Achievement Award

Alumni who demonstrate professional mid-to-late career success and achievement.

Yolanda Armstrong, MSSA 1994
Rene Barrat-Gordon, MSSA 1979
Eva Beard, MSSA 1967
Ralph Belk, MSSA 1996

Patrick Boyle, MSSA 1989, PhD 2016
Phyllis Brody, MSSA 1958
Mark Chapin, PhD 1995
Dabney Conwell, MSSA 2007
Amy S. D'Aprix, PhD 2005
Florence Drage, MSSA 1979
Cynthia Dunn, MSSA 1982
Rachel Foster, MSSA 1997
Joel Fox, MSSA 1980
Michael Freas, MSSA 1975
Darlene Grant, MSSA 1984
Lynn Heemstra, MSSA 1982
Laura Hokenstad, MSSA 1996
Ronald Hughes, MSSA 1975
Vivian Jackson, PhD 2008
Charles "Chip" Joseph, MSSA 1987
Mary Jane Karger, MSSA 1969
Ferne Katleman, MSSA 1957
Shirley Keller, MSSA 1981, PhD 1999
John Lisy, MSSA 1977
Nancy Lowrie, MSSA 1995
Victoria Marion, MSSA 2003
Toby Martin, MSSA 1998, PhD 2007
Karen McHenry, MSSA 1994
Barbara Obiaya, MSSA 1976
Judith Phoenix, MSSA 1968
Jerome "Jerry" Rauckhorst, MSSA 1976
Candace Risen, MSSA 1971
Jane Robertson, MSSA 1995
Philip Starr, MSSA 1959
Kathleen Stoll, MSSA 1960
Alida Struze, MSSA 1959
An-Pyng Sun, PhD 1987

Nonprofit Leadership Award

Alumni who have been working as leaders for 15 or more years in the nonprofit profession and have earned a Master of Nonprofit Organizations (MNO) degree or a Certificate in Nonprofit Management (CNM).

Sheryl Aikman, MNO 1995

April Alvis, MNO 1999

Marcella Brown, MNO 2007

Mary Anne Crampton, CNM 2007

Eric Dicken, MNO 2009

Phyllis "Seven" Harris, MNO 2005

Timothy Logan, MNO 1994

Ann Lucas, MNO 2000

Marsha Mockabee, CNM 1994

Megan O'Bryan, MNO 1995

Darlene Rebello-Rao, MNO 1998

Scott Simon, MNO 1998

JoAnn White, MNO 1999

Early Career Success

Alumni who demonstrate early career success and achievement.

Miriam Ampeire, MSSA 2009

Matthew Butler, MSSA 2010

Devon Fegen-Herdman, MSSA 2005

Annette Iwamoto, MSSA 2012

Ijeoma Mba, MSSA 2013

Mary McNamara, MSSA 2003

Thomas Mulloy, MSSA 2006

Catherine Rotolo, MSSA 2007

Nathan Schaefer, MSSA 2005

Christa Sharpe, MSSA 2005

Louis Stokes Community Service Leadership Award

Alumna/us who embodies the socially-minded characteristics of the late beloved and honorable Congressman Louis Stokes, including community service, leadership, social justice advocacy, and Mandel School volunteerism and community-related projects support.

Magda Gomez, MSSA 2004

+ 100 Centennial Alumni Award winners congregate for an historic photo with Dean Gilmore *(School Archives)*.

ALUMNI PROFILE:
Ijeoma Mba, MSSA 2013

Mba's personal motto is "Don't confuse the difficult with the impossible." She is a Program Associate at Reboot in Nigeria, a non-governmental organization dedicated to inclusive development and accountable governance. Mba is working to further its programmatic work, particularly in West Africa, by supporting field research, business development, and social impact.

She also works with Road Preppers, which is creating Nigeria's largest community-based trip planner mobile app. As a 2015-16 Global Health Corps Fellow at the Foundation for Community Development in Kasese, Uganda, Mba focused on promoting global health equity to address extreme disparities in health outcomes and access to health care.

She also supported community-based organizations in tackling management challenges and implementing sustainable development projects ranging from agro-processing to improving communications systems for isolated rural communities. Her work has extended across Rwanda and South Africa, focusing on women's rights and online citizen engagement campaigning.

Mba has experience advising, evaluating and implementing community-led development initiatives in the health and governance sectors.

+ Ijeoma Mba, MSSA 2013.

studying issues surrounding aging internationally, was made honorary president of the Global Institute of Social Work in 2014–15, and served as an adviser on programs for the aging to the United Nations Development Program in Beijing, China. Faculty members Mark Joseph and Sharon Milligan traveled to Ghana and Cuba, respectively, and developed new study abroad courses for those

nations. In 2015, the Israeli Council of Higher Education's Quality Assessment Division appointed David E. Biegel to the International Quality Assessment Committee, a six-person team that evaluated social work and human services degree programs in that nation.

The Alumni Association helped sponsor the annual Dollars for Scholars Garage Sale, hosted

+ Centennial Salon Series attendees Chris Hall, MSSA 1978, CNM 2001; Glenda Kupersmith, MSSA 1993; Celeste Terry, MSSA 2003; Gloria Crawford, MSSA 1988; Marjorie Moyar, PhD 1982; Gerda Freedheim, MSSA 1974; Sally Breen, MSSA 1970; host Dianne Hunt, MSSA 1967; Zoe Breen Wood, PhD 2012; Hallie Durchslag, MSSA 1999, on June 29, 2015.

alumni events across the United States, and organized a popular Career Connections Night each year that allowed students to "speed-network" with alumni and form connections. In 2015, the Alumni Association created the Alumni Association Awards, now awarded annually. Alumni also participated in the Third Monday events beginning in 2016, where alumni, community practitioners, faculty, and students met for conversations and continuing education on a series of topics.

By 2016, on-campus and online students provided 240,599 hours of service to the community

through their field placements—an economic value of more than $6.3 million. Their activism reached beyond the classroom, as students joined volunteers from the School of Medicine and the Francis Payne Bolton School of Nursing to staff Case Western Reserve's Student-Run Free Clinic (SRFC) beginning in 2013. The Mandel Council for Student Community Leadership, which coordinated stu-

dent activities and ensured student representation on faculty and School committees, was active throughout the 2010s. Mandel Council organized student events, presented awards, participated in industry events, and streamlined communication between the School and students. Other student groups included the Mandel Allies, the Black Student Association (BSA), Local INternational Konnec-

ENDOWED DEANSHIP
Jack, Joseph and Morton Mandel Dean
in Applied Social Sciences

ENDOWED PROFESSORSHIPS
Grace Longwell Coyle Professor in Social Work
Henry L. Zucker Professor of Social Work
Leonard W. Mayo Professor in Family and
    Child Welfare
Lillian F. Harris Professor of Urban
    Research & Social Change
Dr. Semi J. and Ruth W. Begun Professor
Ralph S. and Dorothy P. Schmitt Professor
Verna Houck Motto Professor of Families
    and Communities
Leona Bevis/Marguerite Haynam Professor
    in Community Development

+ Mandel Council leadership in 2016: Amarinder Syan, Kaitlyn Uhl, Jenn Angelo, Jazmin Danner, Janelle Duda, and Samia Mansour.

+ 2015–2016 faculty: Sharon Milligan, Rashonda Clay-Douthit, David Crampton, Zoe Breen Wood, Sherlina L. Thomas, Scott A. Wilkes, Gerald Strom, Deborah Jacobson, Regina Nixon, Victor Groza, Nancy Neuer, Cristina Nedelcu, Meeyoung Min, Sonia Minnes, David Biegel, Francisca Cobian-Richter, Stephanie Gilman, Dean Grover C. Gilmore, Richard Romaniuk, Sarah Andrews, David Hussey, Marjorie Edguer, Aloen Townsend, Kathleen Farkas, Kathi Overmier-Gant, Laura A. Voith, David Miller, Elizabeth Anthony, Gerald Mahoney, Mark Chupp, Daniel Flannery, Kimberly McFarlin, Beth Brindo, Jody Timko, Lori Longs Painter, LaShon Sawyer, Jennifer A. King, Megan R. Holmes, Dana Prince, Susan Snyder, Mark Joseph, Jeff Kretschmar, Mark Singer, Amy Korsch-Williams, Andrea Porter, Rob Fischer, and former Dean M.C. "Terry" Hokenstad *(Rob Muller)*.

tions (LINK), Student Leaders Advocating for Mental Health (SLAM), and S.A.F.E. Circle, among others.

As the Jack, Joseph and Morton Mandel School of Applied Social Sciences celebrated its centennial, its faculty, students, staff, alumni, and friends honored the School's history and continued to shape its future. Created in response to the request of Cleveland's philanthropic organizations, who needed trained professional social workers to help serve the community, the Mandel School has continually combined cutting edge university-based research with practical field experience. Today, the Mandel School continues to demonstrate leadership in groundbreaking research and teaching, create new educational models, and serve the community through programs and community partnerships.

As the Mandel School enters its second century, it remains strongly committed to its mission of "advancing leadership in social work and nonprofit education, scholarship, and service to build a more just world." +

+ 2015–2016 Master's students at fall orientation *(Maria Sharron)*.

HALL OF ACHIEVEMENT

The newly-established Mandel School Hall of Achievement was founded during the Centennial to recognize the accomplishments of outstanding alumni, faculty, partners, and friends who have greatly impacted the school and the fields of social work or nonprofit management for the past 100 years. These individuals have received school awards, major Case Western Reserve University acknowledgments, or top industry honors.

Margaret E. Adams, MSSA 1944
Sheryl Aikman, MNO 1995
Barbara Munroe Allan, PhD 1991
Margaret Allen
April Alvis, MNO 1999
Goldie Alvis, MSSA 1973
Miriam Ampeire, MSSA 2009
Joseph P. Anderson, MSSA 1932
Sarah S. Andrews, MSSA 1991
Georgia Anetzberger, MSSA 1980, PhD 1986
Yolanda Armstrong, MSSA 1994
Lowell Arye, MSSA 1982
Paula Atwood, MSSA 1973
Sarah Short Austin, MSSA 1962
David M. Austin, MSSA 1948
Hoda Badran, DSW 1967
Darlyne Bailey
Myrna Balk, MSSA 1963
Charles A. Ballard, MSSA 1972
Olive K. Banister, Ex-MSSA 1935
Rene BarratGordon, MSSA 1979
Mildred C. Barry, MSSA 1935
Jennifer M. Bartholomew, PhD 2015
Marcus Battle, MSSA1950
Eva Beard, MSSA1967
Ralph Belk, MSSA 1996
David Bergholz
Philip Bernstein, MSSA1934
Margaret Berry, MSSA 1937

Leona Bevis, MSW 1943
David E. Biegel
James Billups, MSSA 1954
Clark W. Blackburn, MSSA1935
Eileen Blackey, DSW 1956
Mary Blake, MSA 1934
Arthur Blum, PhD 1960, MSSA 1952
William Thomas Bogart
Margaret F. Bolton, Ex-MSSA 1923
Patrick Boyle, PhD 2016, MSSA 1989
Lawrence Bresler, MSSA1973
Charles D. Brink, MSSW 1941
Margaret Brodkin, MSSA 1967
Grace F. Brody
Phyllis Brody, MSSA 1958
Ralph Brody, PhD 1974, MSSA 1958
Marcella Brown, MNO 2007
Suzanne Brown, PhD 2012
Steve D. Bullock
Geraldine Burns, MSSA 1971
Dorothy Burnside, MSSW 1947
Matthew Butler, MSSA 2010
Jane Campbell, MSSA 1965
Dorothy H. Castle, Ex-MSSA 1919
Margaret L. Celeste, MSSA 1936
Fern Chamberlain, MSSA 1935
Mark Chapin, PhD 1995
Pranab Chatterjee
Patricia M. Choby, MNO 1991
Mark G. Chupp, PhD 2003
Norris E. Class, MSSA 1931
Richard J. Clendenen, MSSW 1947
Richard J. Cloward
Allen Cohen, MSSA 1959
Nathan Cohen
Susan Cole, PhD 2001
Susan A. Comerford, PhD 1998
Dabney Conwell, MSSA 2007
Kevin Conwell
Claudia J. Coulton, PhD 1978
Grace Longwell Coyle
David S. Crampton
Mary Anne Crampton
Spencer H. Crookes, MSSW 1941

Hope Curfman, MSSA 1942
Anita CurryJackson, MSSA 1970
James E. Cutler
Gurdino G. Dadlani, MSSA 1959
Amy S. D'Aprix, PhD 2005
Jane Daroff, MSSA 1985
Erlynne P. Davis, MSSA 1950
Maureen Dee, MSSA 1978
Eric Dicken, MNO 2009
Roosevelt S. Dickey, MSSA 1937
Florence Drage, MSSA 1979
James Dumpson
Ruth E. Dunkle
Cynthia Dunn, MSSA 1982
Susan Eagan
Joyce Edward, MSSA 1946
Richard L. Edwards, MSSA 1964
Daniel R. Elliott, Jr.
Daniel R. Elliott, Sr. MSA 1943
Charles Emlet, PhD 1998
Theodore Fabian
Hans S. Falck
Art J. Falco
Dorothy Faller, MSSA 1975
Kathleen J. Farkas, PhD 1984
Dean Fazekas, MSSA 1991
Devon FegenHerdman, MSSA 2005
Robert L. Fischer
Raymond Fisher, MSSW 1939
Paula A. Fitzgibbon
Jerry E. Floersch
Rachel Foster, MSSA 1997
Joel Fox, MSSA 1980
Michael Freas, MSSA 1975
Claire E. Freeman
Gerald Futty, MSSA 1958
Angelo J. Gagliardo, MSSA 1939
Ursula M. Gallagher MSA 1938
vic gelb
Karachepone Ninan George, MSSA 1959
Eleanor R. Gerson, MSSA 1966
Denise Gibson, MSSA 1978
Grover "Cleve" Gilmore
Wallace J. Gingerich

Mitchell I. Ginsberg
Stuart Gitlin, MSSA 1973
Howard Goldstein
Magda Gomez, MSSA 2004
Sol Gothard, MSSA 1957
Darlene Grant, MSSA 1984
Jean Greenhaigh
Howard Gustafson MSA 1940
Kirsten M. Hagesfeld, MSSA 1977
Cailen Haggard
Marjorie Hall-Ellis, MSSA1962
Lillian F. Harris, MSSA 1933
Phyllis "Seven" Harris, MNO 2005
Margaret Hartford
Ann Hartman
Lois Hayes
Marguerite Haynam, MSSA 1941
Lynn Heemstra, MSSA 1982
Virginia O. Herbst, MSSA 1935
Frank J. Hertel, MSSA 1934
Stephen H. Hoffman
Laura Hokenstad, MSSA 1996
M.C. Terry Hokenstad
Stanley B. Horowitz, MSSA1959
Ronald Hughes, MSSA 1975
Donald B. Hurwitz, MSW 1937
Annette Iwamoto, MSSA 2012
Hazel C. Jackson, MSSW 1929
Vivian Jackson, PhD 2008
Deborah R. Jacobson
Eliezer Jaffe, DSW 1960, MSSA 1957
Jeffrey Janata
Edmond T. Jenkins, MSSA 1966
Kathryn P. Jensen
Ella Mae Cheeks Johnson, MSSA 1928
Geneva Johnson, MSSA 1957
Margaret H. Johnson, MSSA 1919
Richard Lewis Jones, PhD 1981, MSSA 1975
Charles "Chip" Joseph, MSSA 1992
Mark L. Joseph
Mitchell Kahan
Mary Jane Karger, MSSA 1969
Ferne Katleman, MSSA 1957
Israel Katz, DSW 1962

Robert Keefe, MSSA 1985
Shirley Keller, PhD 1981
Deborah Kendig
Margaret M. Kennedy, MSSA 1978
Anna E. King, MSSA 1926
Lenore A. Kola
Derrick Kranke, PhD 2009
Florence G. Kreech, MSSA 1939
Arthur H. Kruse, MSSA 1942
Margaret Pauline Roney Lang, MSSA 1933
Jean Lawrence, MSSA 1984
India Pierce Lee, MSSA 2005
Marcia Levine, MSSA 1966
Verl S. Lewis, DSW 1954
Art Lifson, MSSA 1969
Mark Light
Belle Likover, MSSA 1969
Wayne Lindstrom, PhD 1986
John Lisy, MSSA 1977
Timothy Logan, MNO 1994
Gail Long, MSSA 1967
Jacalyn Lowe-Stevenson, MSSA 1978
Nancy Lowrie, MSSA 1995
Ann Lucas, MNO 2000
Elizabeth I. Lynch, MSSA 1948
Robert P. Madison
Marjorie W. Main, MSSA 1954
Chris A. Mallett
Salvatore A. Mandalfino, MSSA 1939
Jack N. Mandel
Joseph C. Mandel
Morton L. Mandel
Soad Mansour, MSSA 1972
Victoria Marion, MSSA 2003
Flavio Marsiglia, PhD 1991
Toby Martin, PhD 2007, MSSA1998
John Matsushima, DSW 1963, MSSA1953
Jean Maxwell, MSSA 1941
Leonard W. Mayo
Ijeoma Mba, MSSA 2013
James McCafferty, MSSA 1990
W. Thomas McCullough, MSSA 1933
Karen McHenry, MSSA 1994
Mary McNamara, MSSA 2003

Lillian Milanof, MSSA 1949
David B. Miller
Steven Minter, MSSA 1963
Marsha Mockabee, CNM 1994
Robert Morris, MSSA 1935
Milton C. Morris, MSSA 1975
Eric Morse, MSSA 1998
Kirsti Mouncey
Thomas Mulloy, MSSA 2006
Michelle R. Munson
Myrtle Muntz, MSSA 1964
Michael Murphy, PhD 1974
Meher C. Nanavatty, MS 1950
Arthur Naparstek
Aravindhan Natarajan, PhD 2010
Patricia "Pat" Nobili, MSSA 1983
Barbara Obiaya, MSSA 1976
Tom O'Brien, MSSA 2003
Megan O'Bryan, MNO 1995
Shig Okada, MSSA 1949
Ralph Ormsby, MSSA 1933
Nancy Osgood
Kathi Overmier-Gant, MSSA 1990
Lisa Pape, MSSA 1990
R. Susan Pearlmutter
David Pedlar, PhD 1997
Wilma Peebles-Wilkins, MSSA 1971
Ruby Pernell
Judith Phoenix, MSSA 1968
Norman Polansky, MSSA 1943
Curtis D. Proctor, PhD 2006
Joseph Pyles, MSSA 1952
Steven Raichilson
Jerome "Jerry" Rauckhorst
Darlene Rebello-Rao, MNO 1998
Candace Risen, MSSA 1971
Carol Rivchun
Jane Robertson, MSSA 1995
Jim Rokakis
Jay L. Roney, MSSW 1939
William S. Rooney, DSW 1956
Marvin Rosenberg, PhD 1968, MSSA 1962
Edna Roth, MSSA 1952
Catherine Rotolo, MSSA 2007

H. Ted Rubin, MSSA 1950
Bernard Russell, MSSA 1942
Marian E. Russell, MSW 1930
Janet Sainer, MSSA 1941
Paul Salipante
Nathan Schaefer, MSSA 2005
Nancy Schiffer, MSSA 1971
Lillian Schlachter, MSSA 1976
Roy Schlachter, MSSA 1959
Alvin Schorr
Connie Schultz
Harvey Shankman, MSSA 1974, CNM 1988
Beth Shapiro, MSSA 1996
Christa Sharpe, MSSA 2005
William H. Sheridan, MSSA 1939
Barbara Silverstone
Maya M. Simek, MSSA 2007
Scott Simon, MNO 1998
David A. Simpson, MSSA 1999
Patricia Sinclair
Mark Singer, PhD 1983, MSSA 1979
Seymour Slavin, MSSA 1958
H Bernard Smith, MSSA 1954
John Palmer Smith
Rebecca C. Smith, MSSA 1939
Norman Sohn, MSSA 1968
Phyllis Solomon, PhD 1978, MSSA 1970
Mary Louise Somers, DSW 1957, MSSA 1943
Joan Southgate, MSSA 1954
Harry Specht, MSW 1953
Dorothea Spellman MSA 1933
Philip Starr, MSSA 1959
Herman Stein
Melody Stewart, PhD 2008
Richard O. Stock, MSSA 1939
Louis Stokes
Kathleen Stoll, MSSA 1960
James L. Strachan
Mary Lou Stricklin
Gerald A. Strom
Kimberly Strom-Gottfried
Alida Struze, MSSA 1959
AnPyng Sun, PhD 1987
Ilga Svechs

Hank Tanaka, MSSA 1951
Sachie Tanaka, MSSA 1946
Virginia Sandifer Tannar
Caroline Tempio, MSSA 1951
Celeste Terry, MSSA 2003
Esther I. Test, MSSA 1938
Ella Thomas, MSSA 1971
Maria J. Thompson, MSSA 2005
Toni-Jane Tickton, MSSA 1980
John J. Toner, MSSA 1940
Mario Tonti
Elizabeth M. Tracy
John B. Turner, DSW 1959, MSSA 1948
Barbara K. Varley, DSW 1962
Helen M. Walker, MSSA 1918
John Wallin, MSSA 1995
Creed F. Ward, MSSA 1936
Elizabeth Law Watkins, MSSA 1950
Kathryn S. Weitzel, MSSA 1941
Eleanor Weisberger Weintraub, MSSA 1943
Kathleen Wells
Pearl S. Whitman
Margaret "Margie" Wheeler, MSSA 1970
JoAnn White, MNO 1999
Scott A. Wilkes, PhD 2013
Danny R. Williams, MNO 2004
Joy Willmott
Donald V. Wilson
Zoe Breen Wood, PhD 2012
Judith L. Wylie, MSSA 1935
Gautam Yadama, PhD 1990, MSSA 1985
John A. Yankey
Dennis Young
Henry L. Zucker, MSSA 1935

Acknowledgments

We would like to extend our most sincere thanks to the Jack, Joseph and Morton Mandel Foundation for their generous support of this project.

Thank you to everyone at the Jack, Joseph and Morton Mandel School of Applied Social Sciences and Case Western Reserve University who shared their time and insight, including countless alumni, faculty, staff, and students—many of whom came to life as we pored through bulletins, newsletters, and photos in the School and University archives. Your stories inspired us and truly gave us hope.

We would like to say a special thank you to the following individuals who made themselves available for formal interviews: Morton L. Mandel; Dean Grover C. Gilmore, PhD; former deans Darlyne Bailey, PhD; Wallace Gingerich, PhD; Richard Edwards, PhD; M.C. "Terry" Hokenstad, PhD; and John Yankey, PhD; alumnus Steven Minter, MSSA 1963; and faculty members Lenore A. Kola, PhD, and Sharon Milligan, PhD.

In particular, we must thank our interviewer and research colleague, Shelley Stokes Hammond, an oral historian who conducted each interview with care and copious amounts of background research, gleaning insights nobody else could.

Our gratitude also extends to all of the following individuals, organizations, and committees that supported and assisted the project:

- Centennial Planning Committee and its Co-Chairs: John Yankey, PhD; Kathleen J. Farkas, PhD 1984; and Denise Gibson, MSSA 1978, PhD
- John Grabowski, PhD, Krieger-Mueller Associate Professor of Applied History at Case Western Reserve University and Vice President of Research and Publications at Western Reserve Historical Society
- Richard E. Baznik, Vice President Emeritus and University Historian at Case Western Reserve University
- Jill Tatem and Helen Conger at Case Western Reserve University Archives
- Samantha Skutnik and the team of librarians at the Lillian F. and Milford J. Harris Library
- Thomas Vince at Western Reserve Academy
- *The Plain Dealer*
- The Mandel School's Institutional Advancement team, including Tracey Bradnan, Director of Marketing and Communications; Nada DiFranco, MNO 2008, Director of Alumni Relations; Nora Hennessy, MNO 2004, Associate Dean for Institutional Advancement; Marianne Lax, MSSA 1990, Director of Charitable Giving; and Edna Wade, Department Assistant.
- Student researchers Abby Assmus, MSSA/MA 2017; Katrice Williams, MSSA/MNO 2016; Jennine Vlach, CNM 2012, MNO 2016; Ann Blackman, MSSA/MPH Candidate; and Leah Adams, MSSA/MNO Candidate.

Elise C. Hagesfeld, MNO, PhD
Elizabeth Salem, PhD

Bibliography and Further Reading

ARCHIVES AND ONLINE RESOURCES

Call & Post, Cleveland, Ohio

Case Western Reserve University Archives, Cleveland, Ohio

Cleveland Jewish News, Cleveland, Ohio

Cleveland Memory Project, Cleveland State University, Cleveland, Ohio: http://www.clevelandmemory.org

Cleveland Public Library Digital Gallery, Cleveland Public Library, Cleveland, Ohio: http://cplorg.cdmhost.com/cdm/

Encyclopedia of Cleveland History, Case Western Reserve University, Cleveland, Ohio: https://case.edu/ech

Jack, Joseph, and Morton Mandel School of Applied Social Sciences Archives, Cleveland, Ohio

National Association of Social Workers, Social Work Pioneers, Washington, D.C.: http://naswfoundation.org/pioneer.asp

Ohio History Central, Ohio History Connection, Columbus, Ohio: http://www.ohiohistorycentral.org

The Plain Dealer, Cleveland, Ohio

Rockefeller Archive Center, Sleepy Hollow, New York

Social Welfare History Archives, University of Minnesota Libraries, Minneapolis, Minnesota

Western Reserve Historical Society Archives, Cleveland, Ohio

JOURNALS AND BOOKS

Austin, David M. "The Flexner Myth and the History of Social Work." *Social Service Review* 57, no. 3 (1983): 357–77.

Austin, David M. *A History of Social Work Education.* Austin: School of Social Work, The University of Texas at Austin, 1986.

Austin, David M. "The Institutional Development of Social Work Education: The First 100 Years—and Beyond." *Journal of Social Work Education* 33, no. 3 (1997): 599–612.

Baznik, Richard E. *Beyond the Fence: A Social History of Case Western Reserve University.* Cleveland, OH: Case Western Reserve University, 2014.

Bruno, Frank J. "Twenty-Five Years of Schools of Social Work." *Social Service Review* 18, no. 2 (1944): 152–64.

Bruno, Frank J. *Trends in Social Work as Reflected in the Proceedings of the National Conference of Social Work, 1874-1946.* New York: Columbia University Press, 1948.

Campbell, Thomas F. *SASS: Fifty Years of Social Work Education: A History of the School of Applied Social Sciences, Case Western Reserve University.* Cleveland: Press of Case Western Reserve University, 1967.

Coyle, Grace Longwell. *Studies in Group Behavior.* New York, NY: Harper & Brothers, 1937.

Cutler, James Elbert, and Maurice R. Davie. *A Study in Professional Education at Western Reserve University, the School of Applied Social Sciences, 1916-1930.* Cleveland: Western Reserve University Press, 1930.

Dulmus, Catherine N., and Karen M. Sowers. *The Profession of Social Work: Guided by History, Led by Evidence.* Hoboken, N.J: Wiley, 2012.

Dunlap, Katherine M. "A History of Research in Social Work Education: 1915-1991." *Journal of Social Work Education* 29, no. 3 (October 1993): 293–301.

Miller, Carol Poh, and Robert A. Wheeler. *Cleveland: A Concise History, 1796-2006. The Encyclopedia of Cleveland History: Illustrated Volumes.* Bloomington, IN: Indiana University Press, 1997.

Newstetter, Wilber I., Marc J. Feldstein, and Theodore M. Newcomb. *Group Adjustment; a Study in Experimental Sociology.* Cleveland, OH: The School of Applied Social Sciences, Western Reserve University, 1938.

Newstetter, Wilber I., and Marc J. Feldstein. *Wawokiye Camp: A Research Project in Group Work.* Cleveland, OH: The School of Applied Social Sciences, Western Reserve University, 1930.

Feldman, Ronald A. "Reputations, Rankings, and Realities of Social Work Schools: Challenges for Future Research." *Journal of Social Work Education* 42, no. 3 (2006): 483–505.

Fisher, Robert. "'Speaking for the Contribution of History': Context and the Origins of the Social Welfare History Group." *Social Service Review* 73, no. 2 (1999): 191–217. doi:10.1086/514414.

Tufts, James Hayden. *Education and Training for Social Work.* New York: Russell Sage Foundation, 1923.

Walker, Sydnor Harbison. *Social Work and the Training of Social Workers.* University of North Carolina. Social Study Series. Chapel Hill: The University of North Carolina Press, 1928.

Index